LOCKHEED
F·117A

Operation and Development of the Stealth Fighter

Bill Sweetman & James Goodall

Motorbooks International
Publishers & Wholesalers ®

*To Ben Rich, leader of the Skunk Works
from 1975 to 1990*

First published in 1990 by Motorbooks International Publishers & Wholesalers, P O Box 2, 729 Prospect Avenue, Osceola, WI 54020 USA

The information in this book is true and complete to the best of our knowledge. All recommendations are made without any guarantee on the part of the author or publisher, who also disclaim any liability incurred in connection with the use of this data or specific details

We recognize that some words, model names and designations, for example, mentioned herein are the property of the trademark holder. We use them for identification purposes only. This is not an official publication

Motorbooks International books are also available at discounts in bulk quantity for industrial or sales-promotional use. For details write to Special Sales Manager at the Publisher's address

Library of Congress Cataloging-in-Publication Data
Sweetman, Bill.
    Lockheed F-117 Stealth fighter / Bill Sweetman, James C. Goodall.
      p. cm.
    ISBN 0-87938-470-0
    1. F-117 (Jet fighter plane)
I. Goodall, James C. II. Title.
UG1242.F5S964 1990 90-33862
358.4′3—dc20   CIP

On the front cover: The Lockheed F-117 looks unique from any angle—especially the front. *USAF photo by Eric Schulzinger of Lockheed*

On the back cover: Lt. Col. Ralph Getchell opens the canopy of his F-117. *James C. Goodall*

Printed and bound in the United States of America

Contents

Acknowledgments

Thanks are, as always, due to my wife, Mary Pat, for her immense tolerance of the mental absences and unrepaired faucet washers that are the domestic price of authorship. Jim "Cookie Monster" Goodall forgot to mention her chocolate-chip cookies in his acknowledgments, so I will do so here. Martin and Evan, who no longer amend my artwork and have even stopped eating snacks on my keyboard—a hug to both of you.

This book has two authors. Without Jim Goodall's untiring research, it would have contained less than half the information that it does. Jim has contributed a great deal in the past to many books, including some of mine, and I am very happy that he has at least received the title-page recognition that he deserves.

Bill Sweetman

First and foremost, I want to thank my wife, Shelley, son, James, and daughter, Alicia, for being so very understanding of my passion for Lockheed-built "Black Airplanes." Without their support this project would have never gotten off the ground.

To my coauthor, Bill Sweetman, who really made it happen; to John Andrews of the Testor Corporation, one of my best friends and fellow follower of things that go bump in the night; to John Lear who was kind enough to take me to the Tonopah Test Range northern fence line for the very first time in Nov 1988 to view the F-117A; and the ASI security SWAT team members at Tonopah Test Range who were so very kind to me during my six visits to the fence line.

To Ben R. Rich, Vice President and General Manager of the Lockheed Skunk Works, who was forbidden by security constraints and requirements to offer any direct help; I thank him for his emotional support over the years.

To the men who helped me behind the scenes that must remain anonymous, thank you.

To a young and very talented photographer, Tony Landis, whose help I can't measure; to the man who taught me how to shoot a camera, Charles B. Mayer; to Jay Miller of Aerofax who always has supported my love for black airplanes; Mike Dornheim of *Aviation Week;* to Marty Isham, a good friend and fellow airplane shooter; and to Lt. Chris Mayer, a young man who shares the same love for airplanes as his dad and I. To Maj. Gen. Wayne C. Gatlin, Minnesota ANG, Ret., the best boss a Guardsman ever had; to fellow photographers and friends who, over the years, never got tired of my love for black airplanes; Maj. Brian (Buck) Rogers; Dave Prettyman; Randy Kovisko; Doug Slowiak; Kevin Patrick; Robert Arance; James Bamford; James Eastham, (retired A–12/SR–71 pilot); Jeff Ethell who really got me started as a writer; Mick Roth; James Perry Stevenson; to Col. Tony Tolin, Commander of the 37th TFW; TSgt Bobby Sheldon, 37th TFW/PA; Col. Sconyers and LTC Weber both of TAC Headquarters who, along with the staff of the 57th FFW/PA at Nellis AFB, NV, and the members of the 37th TFW, made the first media and public showing of the F–117A such a success.

I thank you all.

Jim Goodall

Introduction

Stealth broke into the national press in the summer of 1986, after an F–117A crashed in California. Other reporters started to call me. As a matter of professional competence, reporters have to be better informed about national events than the average person; but many of the voices on the other end of the phone had never heard of the Stealth Fighter, much less of the billions of dollars that the US Government had spent to build a whole squadron of the aircraft. Because, of course, it was secret.

As you read this book, bear in mind that, at the time that most of the events which it covers took place, the US government would not admit that the F–117A even existed. Remember, too, that the secret military extends well beyond the Stealth Fighter.

We all know, for example, that the United States uses reconnaissance satellites to gather information about its adversaries; however, what we know about these satellites has been dug out by reporters and writers, and the Pentagon itself has never released one word of information, not even on the oldest satellites.

One sad effect of all this secrecy is that it deprives some remarkable people of their due. When the media are sated with celebrities, they exalt windbag politicians and paper billionaires. As we write, the two highest-rated "realistic" TV drama series focus on the agonized lives of top-dollar lawyers and advertising account executives.

This is the story of how real engineers and pilots offered and sometimes gave everything they had, re-invented the military aircraft and helped to change the world. If one bright young person decides that it sounds more interesting than serving writs or creating concepts for pet food conglomerates, it was worth the telling.

Chapter 1

A quiet place in the mountains

"I didn't keep a diary, because I never thought anyone would ever give a damn."

A Skunk Works engineer

Groom Lake, Nevada, is nobody's idea of a place where history should be made. Walled off from the outside world by the desert mountains of the Timpahute and Pahranagat ranges, and by the Switzerland-sized expanse of closed government land that surrounds it to the south and west, the Groom facility is a makeshift assembly of hangars and supporting buildings. When the desert wind picks up speed across the bone-dry lake, grit the size of quarter-inch rocks blows through the base. Nobody lives there; temporary quarters comprise trailers and some housing of World War II vintage, roughly converted into quarters which allow sleeping and cooking. One of its early nicknames, "The Ranch," was a contraction of the satirical "Paradise Ranch." When a crisis hits and the week-long shifts at Groom stretch into two or three weeks, or even into months, veteran engineers have been known to weep in their supervisors' offices.

It was on a brisk desert winter day, in late January or early February of 1978—the precise date is classified—that Groom's public address system crackled with an unambiguous order: anyone who was not accessed into the *Have Blue* program, anyone who did not have an officially approved need to know what that cryptic phrase involved, should proceed at this time to the cafeteria and stay there until the doors were unlocked. On the ramp, a T–38 trainer stood ready, in case radar operators at Groom detected any unauthorized aircraft approaching the closed airspace around the lake.

Once the area was confirmed as secure, hangar doors opened and a small aircraft, no bigger than the T–38, was towed into the light. A strange machine, with a near-delta wing planform, inward-canted fins, weird gridded inlets, and a cockpit resembling that of a Polish crop-dusting plane, it was quite unlike the powerful and graceful aircraft that had put Groom Lake on the map of aerospace history. Anyone could have told you that it was neither the highest-flying aircraft in the world, as the U-2 had been in its time, nor was it the fastest, like the A-12, forerunner of the Blackbird.

First flight

The *Have Blue* prototype, instead, was designed to be inconspicuous; to sneak into hostile territory undetected by radar, leaving a minimal trace of noise or heat in its wake. The idea was formally known as "low observables" but its more common, shorter and pungently Anglo-Saxon name was Stealth. Most aerospace engineers at the time would have told you without the slightest hesitation that it could not be done, and that, although it might be possible to build an aircraft which would be slightly less easy to spot on radar than a normal design, improvements in radar would soon catch up with it and the airplane would probably not be able to perform a useful military mission. Those who knew better were few, they made no effort to enlighten their professional colleagues, and most of them were at Groom Lake that day.

Many of the team of engineers who watched as the *Have Blue* was inspected and prepared for flight had been together since the U-2 and A-12 days.

Bill Park, the first pilot to fly the Have Blue Stealth *prototype, boards a U-2R for a test flight, probably in the late 1960s.* Lockheed

They were a close-knit, elite unit; each one had been hand-picked and all had been proven through tough projects. They had built aircraft that flew higher and faster than any others, by margins that were classified and much larger than most people believed. They built aircraft faster than any other organization. They usually delivered on time, or early, and on or below cost, and under an impenetrable shroud of secrecy.

One of the veterans was a fifty-one-year-old pilot, William C. Park. A senior test pilot since the late 1950s, Bill Park would have been a legend had he been allowed to tell half his stories. Once, he had landed a U-2 dead-stick at Lockheed's headquarters at Burbank, California, after mechanics had forgotten to open some fuel-transfer valves and the engine flamed out. Park missed the fence and disaster by inches. One of the senior engineers ran to the aircraft and asked him what had happened. "I don't know," responded Park. "I just got here."

Twice, Park had ejected from disabled A-12 prototypes, both times at the absolute limits of the performance of the ejection seat: once at low altitude, on the approach to Groom Lake, and once at high speed over the California coast, after a D-21 drone, launched from the A-12, had suffered a control failure and pitched down into the mother ship, breaking its back. In the second incident, Park's back-seater had also left the aircraft successfully, but drowned before he could be rescued.

"I knew that despite the cold logic and calm dispassion of scientific theory, things can—and do—go wrong between the blueprint perfection of an aircraft when she is on the ground, and that same aircraft once she is airborne." A British test pilot, Bill Waterton, wrote those words in the mid-1950s, describing his approach to a maiden flight. Bill Park and any other test pilot would probably echo them.

Park completed preflight checks, closed the big, clumsy-looking canopy and taxied out to the end of Groom's single long runway under the eyes of the engineers. The aircraft started to roll as the building roar of the General Electric J85 engines drifted across the lake to the spectators. Its nose lifted, and Article 1 in the *Have Blue* program (the prototype had no better name) rose into the sky in a long, flat, straight climb. The engineers knew, at least, that *Have Blue* could fly.

The first flight of the *Have Blue* was a critical turning point in the development of a Stealth aircraft. It took place more than forty years after the idea had been put forward, and thirty-five years after the first serious attempt at it had been made.

Radar

Radar has been decisive in military aviation since the first practical systems were put into use in the late 1930s. Before radar, theorists such as Italy's General Guilio Douhet had argued that there was no practical defense against a massed bomber raid; the bombers would be overhead and attacking as soon as they could be detected, and long gone before fighters could climb to meet them. But radar's first use was to provide early warning of a bombing raid, together with information as to the raid's strength, speed and track. Within a few years, radar was also being used to aim accurate ground-based cannon against airborne targets by day or by night, to allow fighter pilots to start and even complete engagements against targets they need never see, and to guide experimental surface-to-air missiles.

Aircraft designers and air forces have taken equally large steps to negate radar, whether the objective has been to deprive the enemy of early warning or to prevent radar-guided weapons from operating accurately. Most military aircraft carry some kind of radar warning system, which warns the crew that they have been detected. Virtually all front-line combat aircraft carry active noise or deception jammers and chaff dispensers to protect them from radar-guided missiles. More powerful jammers are installed on special-purpose aircraft which either accompany the attacking force or stand off behind the battle area.

Aircraft design to avoid radar does not just mean Stealth. Some combat aircraft, such as the F-111, B-1 and Tornado, are designed from the ground up to avoid radar by flying at very low level. They are concealed from most ground-based radars by the terrain and by the curvature of the Earth.

A complete class of missiles has been developed to home in on radar emissions, either destroying the radar or forcing its operators to stop transmitting. These can be ground-launched, carried for self-defense by strike aircraft or bombers, or carried on specialized defense-suppression aircraft such as the US Air Force's F-4G Wild Weasel.

Compared with this arsenal of weapons and technology, the idea of making the aircraft less detectable by radar in the first place seems so logical that it is not immediately obvious why it is only now being put into practice.

Early attempts at Stealth

The idea of radar camouflage is almost as old as radar itself. The first serious attempt to produce a warplane that would be significantly less visible to radar was made in 1943; and the idea of reducing the radar reflectivity of an aircraft was the subject of a great deal of research between the end of World War II and the early 1970s.

Sir Robert Watson-Watt, the pioneer of British radar, noted as early as 1935 that it would be logical for future heavy bombers to be designed so as to reduce their radar reflectivity. He was generally ignored. Most aircraft designers, at that time, did not even know how to measure the reflectivity of their aircraft.

Radar engineers, however, observed that their radars would detect targets at greater or lesser ranges, depending on the type of aircraft and the angle at which the radar beam struck it. During World War II, experiments were conducted to measure and plot the radar return from different targets. From this, the researchers derived a measurement for radar cross section (RCS), comparing the strength of the return from the target with that of a simple reflective sphere with a one-square-meter cross section.

The first aircraft designers to realize that differences in reflectivity could be tactically useful, and to attempt to reduce reflectivity in an aircraft design, were the brothers Walter and Reimar Horten in Germany. The Hortens, like Jack Northrop in the United States, were apostles of the flying wing, which they considered to be the ultimate aircraft configuration. It is probable that, like Northrop, they initially seized on the flying wing's inherently low radar reflectivity to help sell their ideas to skeptical officials.

In 1943, the Horten brothers designed a twin-jet flying-wing bomber and reconnaissance aircraft. Because of the shortage of materials, tools and workers, a new aluminum aircraft from a virtually unknown team had little chance of being approved for development in Germany. The Hortens proposed to build the new aircraft out of wood, with a central steel-tube subframe; but the skins were to be made of two layers of thin plywood, sandwiched around a core made of glue, sawdust and charcoal. The sole purpose of the charcoal was to absorb radar waves.

As it was eventually tested in 1944, the Horten HoIX had a conventional, non-absorbent plywood skin; but its design embodied a vital truth that was to elude designers until the late 1950s.

During and after the war, researchers in America, Britain and Germany continued to work on radar-absorbent material (RAM). Some types of RAM were used operationally by the German Navy, to shield the snorkel tubes of submarines from Allied airborne radars. In America, by 1945, a team at the Massachusetts Institute of Technology (MIT) Radiation Laboratory had developed an "anti-radar paint" called MX–410. Actually a rubber material containing disc-like aluminum flakes, MX–410 proved to be an effective absorber even in small layers.

Other rubber-based absorbers were developed by divisions of tire companies such as Goodyear and BF Goodrich. Some were produced in forms suitable for airborne use, and, in the 1950s, some

aircraft were treated with RAM and tested against air-defense radars.

The results were invariably disappointing, showing that the RCS reductions which could be achieved by applying RAM to a conventional aircraft were generally insignificant or inconsistent. Given the trial-and-error nature of the tests, this was not surprising. Techniques for modeling and analyzing the radar returns produced by complex, real-world objects were inadequate, and designers did not realize that physically small parts of an aircraft could be disproportionately large radar reflectors.

"Kelly" Johnson and the Skunk Works

In the late 1950s, some designers rediscovered the truth on which the Horten brothers had stumbled: that both shape and RAM are essential if a tactically useful RCS reduction is to be achieved. Aircraft manufacturers developed disciplined approaches to RCS control. They devised ways of predicting the RCS of a new design before it was built. The first RCS ranges were built, so that RCS predictions could be checked before an aircraft was built. Some companies established internal departments to develop specialized forms of RAM, and developed relationships with a growing group of companies specializing in radar/absorber technology.

One of the leaders in this new discipline was Lockheed's Advanced Development Projects (ADP) division, under the leadership of its founder, Clarence L. "Kelly" Johnson.

Johnson had joined Lockheed in 1933, as the company blossomed from a Depression-wracked shell into an industry giant. As the senior assistant to chief engineer Hall Hibbard, Johnson was responsible for the shape of the radical twin-boomed P–38 Lightning fighter and the elegant Constellation transport. In 1943, he was given sole charge of a secret, high-priority project: the development of the United States' first practical jet fighter.

XP-80

The first US jet, the lackluster Bell XP–59A Airacomet, had flown with two early British engines, but in 1943 the British agreed to supply prototypes of new engines in the 4,000–pound-thrust class. Lockheed was given the contract to build the new XP–80 fighter to use the more powerful engine. The engines would arrive within months, and the USAAF was impatient.

Rather than commandeering a complete division, Johnson picked 120 of Lockheed's best design engineers, test engineers, prototype-shop workers and fitters. Part of a production building was screened off from the main plant with wood from old engine crates and was declared off-limits to virtually everyone, irrespective of rank. Each day, Johnson reported briefly to Hibbard on progress, problems and needs, and to a six-man project office at the USAAF Aviation Material Command at Wright Field.

Johnson's team produced the XP–80, from first drawings to first flight, in 143 days. When the USAAF decided that the production version should be bigger, to accommodate the new General Electric TG–180 (J33) engine, the team performed a complete redesign and (doubtless with the aid of practice) produced the YP–80A in 132 days.

Around that time, the hugely popular comic strip *Li'l Abner* was featuring a foul-smelling mountain moonshine still which produced the secret "Essence of Skonk." Johnson's prototype shop first became known as the "Skonk Works"; later, the conventional spelling "Skunk Works" came into use. Despite official disapproval, the name stuck. Johnson used the same technique and many of the same people to produce a series of Lockheed prototypes, including the XF–90 long-range fighter and the F–94, a P–80 modified as a night fighter.

XF-104

Late in 1952, after Johnson had toured Korean fighter bases, the Skunk Works designed and built Lockheed's first supersonic fighter. Compared with its contemporaries, which were either heavy interceptors or fighter-bombers, the XF–104 was light and simple. It was also extremely fast, either in level flight or in a climb, and it was radical in its design; the tiny wings each measured only 7.5 feet from root to tip, were in no place thicker than a large book, and could not have lifted the fighter at any reasonable speed without a specially developed flap blowing system.

The Starfighter, as the F–104 was eventually named, established some Skunk Works traditions. Its performance was well ahead of its contemporaries. Its design was unusual, and it was controversial: the F–104 could be an unforgiving aircraft in a crisis. Also, it was created in complete secrecy and was not unveiled officially until February 1956, two years after its first flight. By that time, the Skunk Works had—literally—gone on to higher things.

U-2

In November 1954, the Skunk Works started the detail design of a high-altitude reconnaissance aircraft for the Central Intelligence Agency (CIA). As yet unnamed, the first "flight article" produced under project *Aquatone* made its first flight on August 4 the following year. It later received the misleading designation U-2, and the first batch comprised twenty aircraft: the first aircraft to be built in quantity by the Skunk Works.

The U-2 was developed under even tighter security than the XF-104. Only those with "need to know"—and they were few—knew it existed. The funding was concealed within the CIA's enormous secret budget.

The U-2's mission was secret and illegal. Security required unusual precautions, in the absence of the wartime censor. Given the climate of relations between East and West, and the McCarthy-era obsession with spies and spying, it would not have taken a genius to guess the most likely mission of a small jet aircraft with long, slender wings for high-altitude performance. The CIA decided to test the U-2 outside the field of view of a casual observer. The site chosen was a dry lake bed in Nevada, next to an old Army station, in an area which had already been declared off-limits to the public because of its proximity to the Nevada nuclear testing sites.

The U-2's mission was to penetrate Soviet airspace and to photograph the most sensitive military sites: missile and

Kelly Johnson and one of the first batch of U-2s. The aircraft carries one of a group of civilian registration numbers that were used to cover the CIA ownership of these aircraft. Lockheed

nuclear weapon test facilities, aircraft factories and bomber bases. The Soviet air defense forces were under orders to destroy unauthorized intruders without warning. The U–2, however, was designed to trespass with impunity, by flying more than two miles above the ceiling of any Soviet fighter.

Today, the U–2 is best remembered for being shot down, but the destruction of Francis Gary Powers' U–2 near Sverdlovsk on May 1, 1960, ended a four-year period in which the CIA's small force of U–2s, packing high-resolution cameras, had roamed at will over the Soviet Union. As an intelligence program, *Aquatone* was a standout success.

A–12

Nobody believed that there were any physical obstacles to developing a fighter or missile which could destroy the U–2. Ways of improving its survivability or producing a better replacement were under study before its first overflight.

One of these was an attempt to make the U–2 less visible on radar, with a combination of Emerson & Cuming Eccosorb radar absorber bonded to the lower fuselage and Salisbury-screen absorbers attached to the fuselage sides. The results were disappointing. The absorbent material provided a relatively small reduction in RCS, but its weight and drag (the modified aircraft was known as "the dirty bird") sharply reduced the U–2's altitude and range performance. Overall, it would have been more, rather than less, vulnerable to attack.

The other way to continue the manned overflight program was to replace the U–2. Its ceiling was near the limit of what could be achieved by a sub-sonic aircraft. The only way to go higher was to go much faster. In an attempt to produce a supersonic replacement for the U–2, Lockheed designed and started to build the CL–400, a massive aircraft fueled by liquid hydrogen. It was abandoned when its range fell short of expectations. Both the attempt to reduce the RCS of the U–2 and the development of the CL–400 were terminated in 1957.

Skunk Works studies of follow-on reconnaissance aircraft began to focus on both high Mach/high altitude and RCS control. When, in 1958, the CIA formally called for a U–2 replacement, Lockheed responded with an aircraft in which, for the first time, a properly designed low-RCS configuration was combined with the use of RAM. In August 1959, Lockheed's A–12 design was selected for development. It made its first flight, from Groom Lake, on April 26, 1962, and fifteen were built for the CIA. Once again, the mere existence of the program—codenamed *Oxcart*—was secret.

Low-RCS features of the A–12 included its slender side profile (the deepest point of the fuselage was at the cockpit, and was no deeper than necessary to accommodate the seated pilot) and the complete elimination of vertical flat surfaces. The sides of the body were flared outward into broad chines, which both helped to lift the aircraft and avoided reflections caused by a conventional rounded body; the same treatment was applied to the outer edges of the engine nacelles. The vertical fins were angled sharply inward.

From above or below, the A–12's aerodynamic shape consisted of a few straight lines and some curves, with no sharp corners except at the engine inlets.

A radar, however, saw something different: the titanium structure of the A–12, on the leading edge of the wing and along the chines, was ringed with large saw-tooth indentations which were carefully shaped and angled to deflect radar signals away from the transmitter. The notches were filled by "pie panels," comprising one-fifth of the surface area and made from a specially developed high-temperature plastic. Finally, the A–12 was coated with a special paint known as "iron ball," containing minute particles of radar-absorbent carbonyl iron material.

The A–12 was one of the first aircraft to undergo RCS model testing, in which a model was placed on a RAM-covered pylon and illuminated with radar at different angles and wavelengths. The tests showed that the new aircraft would have a head-on RCS of only 0.015 square meters, about one-thirtieth that of a conventional fighter. While the aircraft could still be detected by radar, warning times would be greatly reduced, and with the A–12 approaching at Mach 3.5 and 95,000 feet, the defenders would have very little time to mount an effective response. From the rear, the A–12's round, open, titanium and steel jet nozzles presented an enormous radar and infra-red target—but the weapon that can kill an A–12 in a tail-chase has not yet been invented.

For two reasons, the A–12's Stealth features turned out to be largely academic. It never penetrated the world's deepest and toughest air defenses, those of the Soviet Union, because the United States abandoned manned overflights after the U-2 shootdown. (It was a lesser sacrifice than it seemed, because practical reconnaissance satellites were entering service.) Outside the Soviet Union, the A–12 flew high and fast enough to negate any defensive system. The only weapon that posed a real threat to the aircraft was the Soviet S-200 missile (known to the West as the SA-5), and even that Mach-5 monster would not get close enough to destroy the A–12 with a non-nuclear warhead.

SR-71

When Lockheed built a heavier two-seat version of the A–12 for the US Air Force, low-observable characteristics were actually sacrificed to improve its military usefulness; conventional metal-structured chines, incorporating weapon and equipment bays, replaced the absorbent structure. The USAF version was ordered as the experimental YF-12, a test-bed for an advanced interceptor, and the RS-71 reconnaissance-strike aircraft. High-level distaste for the manned bomber resulted in the latter being used exclusively for strategic reconnaissance, as the SR-71, and it was never tested with weapons.

Lockheed was not the only company to explore this first generation of Stealth technology. General Dynamics (GD), which had been the runner-up in the contest to replace the U-2, built one of the first RCS testing ranges and used it to test models of its TFX proposal, which became the F-111. (The F-111's underwing inlets, which later caused no end of aerodynamic problems, may have emerged from these efforts.) GD was then contracted by The USAF to build RATSCAT, the world's biggest RCS range, near Holloman AFB in New Mexico. These were large and costly installations, because the radar had to be far enough away from the model to produce near-parallel beams at the model location; RATSCAT incorporated a mile of perfectly-graded ground between the radar and the pylon.

Ryan Aeronautical (later renamed Teledyne-Ryan) proposed a low-RCS reconnaissance drone in 1960, with such features as a completely flat underside, angled fins and fuselage sides, and a top-mounted engine installation. It was not built, but Ryan provided the US Air Force with a series of reconnaissance drones based on its Firebee target, which were used over Vietnam and China. The company also built its own RCS range.

Results were good enough to rekindle interest in a larger, more sophisticated reconnaissance drone, ordered in 1966 under the codename *Compass Arrow*. With swept wings spanning 49 feet, and an 8,000-pound-thrust engine, it was not a small aircraft, but a combination of shaping features and built-in RAM gave it a commendably low RCS, primarily in the lower microwave frequencies where the acquisition and tracking radars of Soviet-built surface-to-air missile systems operated. During tests of *Compass Arrow*, Teledyne-Ryan and the US Air Force launched one of the drones from its C–130 mother ship over the West Coast and flew it to Washington, DC and back—without detection by civil or military surveillance radars.

D-21

Lockheed developed another low-RCS unmanned vehicle for strategic reconnaissance. Under a still-highly-classified program, initially known as *Tagboard*, the Skunk Works developed a drone of extraordinary performance. Despite its size—it weighed some 13,000 pounds fully fueled—it not only flew faster (Mach 3.8) and higher (100,000 feet)

than the A–12, but it had a greater range, a near-global 15,000 miles. This was the D–21, and very little has been published about it, even today.

The D–21 resembled an A–12 nacelle mated to a pair of A–12 outer wings, and used the same shaping techniques to reduce its radar image. It was powered by a single Marquardt RJ43-MA–11 ramjet engine, originally produced for the massive Boeing IM–99 Bomarc surface-to-air missile, which was mated to a carefully tuned inlet and exhaust nozzle.

The D–21 was designed to be launched from a modified A–12. On the seventh test launch, however, the D–21 experienced a power loss (probably the result of an inlet "unstart" or a violent choking of the supersonic flow into the engine), collided with the A–12 and destroyed it. This was the incident from which Bill Park alone escaped.

Analysis showed that the high-speed launch of the D–21 would not be acceptably safe, so the program was redirected toward a more conservative subsonic launch from a B–52H. A solid rocket booster—weighing more than the D–21 itself—was used to accelerate the D–21 to its cruising height and speed.

The B–52H/D–21 combination entered service in late 1969 under the codename *Senior Bowl*, but only five operational missions were attempted before the program was terminated in mid-1973. No useful imagery was obtained, because of problems with navigation and film recovery, and President Richard Nixon's decision to halt drone overflights of China put an end to the mission requirement. The entire program had cost $2 billion (in 1964 money). The *Compass Arrow* program, which had also been undergoing a protracted and difficult development, was terminated at the same time.

The A-12, SR-71 and D-21 projects turned the Skunk Works into a technology powerhouse. From the start of project *Aquatone* until late 1967, when the last of 31 SR-71s was delivered, the Skunk Works had grown almost 100-fold. The team that had built the first *Aquatone* "article" was not much bigger than Johnson's original XP-80 group. The workforce grew as the U-2 went into production; but the U-2, notwithstanding its advanced design, was simple and conventional from the structural and systems viewpoints. The first batch was built in a small factory near Bakersfield.

The abortive hydrogen-fueled CL-400 was much bigger and more complex, and demanded a further expansion of the Skunk Works' engineering force. In 1958, as design work advanced on the A-12, the Skunk Works was formally named as the Advanced Development Projects (ADP) division of Lockheed-California.

While the U-2 was elegant in its simplicity, the A-12 was elegantly complex. It was as big as a B-58 Hustler, and it incorporated more simultaneous advances in aerodynamics, stability and control, propulsion, materials, and subsystems than any aircraft before or since. When the A-12 made its first flight, Kelly Johnson remarked, "There goes our $67 million airplane." That $67 million multiplied by fifteen is almost exactly $1 billion, and it is reasonable to assume that $1 billion—in early 1960s dollars—was the approximate cost of developing the A-12 and building fifteen aircraft.

Along with big budgets went a further expansion of the work force. By the mid-1960s, ADP employed 8,000 people and was the largest single part of Lockheed-California. It was also the largest customer for Lockheed's Rye Canyon research center, which had been commissioned at Kelly Johnson's behest in 1958. Rye Canyon's secluded laboratories conducted basic research in materials, aerodynamics and any other technologies that could be needed in the future. But two features still distinguished the Skunk Works from other military aircraft design and production organization around the country, despite its growth: its unique management style and its ability to maintain secrecy.

In a nominally open society, what ADP has concealed is hardly believable. The existence of the A-12, for example, remained secret for almost twenty-three years; it was revealed just before the twentieth anniversary of its first flight. Photos of the YF-12 fighter (deliberately misidentified as the non-existent A-11) were released in February 1964; the SR-71's existence was revealed a few months later. But the billion-dollar program to build fifteen single-seat spyplanes for the CIA went completely unreported.

Ben Rich takes the reins

Rich has been with the Skunk Works since the days of the U-2; he was in charge of propulsion and thermodynamic systems, and was instrumental in developing the A-12 propulsion system. He is forceful, energetic and opinionated—characteristics which he shares with every successful design team leader since Wilbur Wright.

As the leader of the world's most respected design team, Rich is in a good position to speak his mind. He casti-

Ben Rich was Johnson's leading assistant in the development of the SR–71 Blackbird and has headed the Skunk Works since 1975. Lockheed

gates bureaucrats for creating "UFOs— Un-Funded Opportunities." He was never too pleased about the Pentagon's refusal even to test air-to-surface weapons on the SR–71: "We gave away the high ground." At a conference on future supersonic transports in 1986, Rich described the idea of a Mach 5 SST as "bull-sauce" and proceeded to demolish the concept in five minutes of well-chosen argument.

Ben Rich sums up the "real secret of the Skunk Works" in one word: "Creativity. We have a lot of people in the Skunk Works whom I call mavericks. They're not afraid to break convention." It is not a bad description of Rich himself.

The organization that Ben Rich took over from its creator, in 1975, was not overworked. Production of the SR–71 and the second-generation U–2R had been completed long before. The USAF had turned down a proposed new version of the F–104, the Lockheed CL–1200 Lancer. Serious design work had been undertaken on a manned hypersonic research aircraft, the X–24C- L301, which would have been launched, like the D–21, from the back of an A–12. It became one of Ben Rich's UFOs.

Stealth revival

Rich placed more emphasis than Johnson on the arcane science of Stealth. Like most chief designers, Johnson was an aerodynamicist by background and inclination, and electrical engineering held little interest for him. "If Kelly could have found a hydraulic radio, he would have used it," a Skunk Works insider has observed.

The mid-1970s saw a Stealth revival. The RCS reductions which had been achieved in the A-12 and D-21 proved that the first-generation RCS measurement ranges, "iron ball" paint and RCS-reducing design techniques all worked as they were supposed to. With this knowledge in hand, engineers could push Stealth technology harder in an all-new design.

In 1975, the USAF convened its first Radar Camouflage Symposium at Wright-Patterson AFB, Ohio. It was a sign that military aviators were ready to look at a new concept that might protect them from radar. Before 1965, the total number of USAF aircraft shot down by radar-guided SAMs was two: Francis Powers' U-2, and Major Rudolf Anderson's U-2, shot down over Cuba in October 1962. Three U-2s flown by Chinese Nationalist pilots had been shot down over China. But new strike aircraft such as the F-105 and the brand-new F-111 flew fast and low and carried radar jammers, radar warning equipment and chaff, and were expected to survive.

In 1965, no anti-radiation missiles existed; no specialized defense-suppression aircraft existed; and only a few aircraft were devoted to jamming. All these things were hastily invented in 1966-67 as losses to SA-2 missiles and radar-guided guns began to mount. By 1972, fewer than half the aircraft in a Linebacker strike against North Vietnam carried weapons destined for the primary target. The rest were jammers, Wild Weasel defense-suppression aircraft and chaff-bombers. Worse, events in the following year cast doubt on whether this kind of effort would be enough.

In the October 1973 battles between Israel and Egypt, the latter used the Soviet Union's SA-6 missile in action for the first time. Its tracking radar was different from that used by older Soviet missiles, and Israel's jamming equipment proved to be ineffective. The Israel Defense Force, which had counted on achieving immediate air supremacy over the battlefield, suffered heavy losses of aircraft and lost ground because its strike aircraft could not support its ground forces.

Some military futurists began to question whether the manned aircraft had a future. But engineers and planners familiar with Stealth could see that an aircraft which would be inherently less visible to radar than a conventional aircraft would be safe from all radar-directed threats, present and future, known or unknown. The array of jammers and escort assets developed would not be needed. But the question was whether such an aircraft could be built.

The snag is that radar is a very sensitive long-range detection device. The microwave source that provides the motive power for a modern radar is not particularly large, and most of the power that it produces streams into empty space. Most of the energy that does strike a target is reflected away from the source. From the scintilla of energy that is reflected back toward the radar, however, the system can determine the bearing, elevation and range of the target and, by measuring the rate at which those parameters change, it can compute and display the target's speed and direction of flight.

Radar has been improved over the years, both in power output and in sensitivity. In the 1960s, for example, the traveling-wave tube (TWT) replaced the magnetron as a microwave source, permitting higher power outputs without a proportionate increase in internal electronic noise. Advances in electronic computing permitted better, real-time processing of the radar return, further improving the radar's ability to discriminate between a genuine echo and noise.

On the other side of the equation, the target's reflectivity is also only one of a number of factors that determine the range at which the radar will detect it. Changing the target's RCS does not reduce detection range by an equal amount; in fact, detection range is in proportion to the fourth root of RCS. As a result, RCS must be reduced by a factor of ten to make a significant difference to detection range. A 100–fold RCS reduction seriously hampers the performance of most radars. A thousand-fold reduction is necessary if the aircraft is to penetrate undetected within striking range of a SAM-defended target. The result was that attempts at reducing the RCS of aircraft tended to be outpaced by the development of better radar.

Cracking the Stealth cipher

The 1975 Radar Camouflage Symposium was classified and its proceedings have not been released. However, it is safe to assume that the symposium included a look back at the Lockheed and Ryan experiments, a review of the state of the art in RAM and a glance at the projected development of the radar threat. Engineers and managers would have left knowing that the USAF was keenly interested in Stealth, but short of ideas on how to achieve massive RCS reductions in a practical aircraft.

The solution to the problem was locked inside a century-old set of equations. James Clerk Maxwell, a Scottish physicist, had derived a set of equations that could predict how a body of a given shape would scatter, or reflect, electromagnetic radiation. For a simple shape—a cone, a sphere or a plane—at a single angle of incidence, Maxwell's equations were readily soluble. But any conceivable, flyable aircraft would be a very complex shape, and the angle at which the radar wave would strike it would change minutely but significantly from one radar sweep to the next. The task of predicting how such a shape would scatter radiation over all feasible angles of incidence was simply beyond human capability.

Two Skunk Works engineers cracked Maxwell's ciphers in 1975. Veteran designer Bill Schroeder sketched a flyable, controllable aircraft with no curved surfaces at all, except for small-radius, straight edges to its wings and tail surfaces. It was as if a diamond had been cut to the shape of an aircraft, and the technique came to be called "faceting." From any angle, the faceted aircraft would present a finite number of edges and flat surfaces to the radar wave; computing the total scattering pattern would still be difficult, but it would be far more attainable than attempting to predict scattering from curved surfaces.

Schroeder took the problem to Dennis Overholser, a member of the profession that the world was beginning to call a "software engineer." Using the Skunk Works' Control Data mainframe computer, Overholser developed a program which could model the scattering from Schroeder's new faceted shapes, and predict their RCS, in a reasonable amount of time.

Now, the designer could produce a shape which looked as though it would fly and manage incoming radar energy at the same time; the computer would show him how well it would work, and if it did not, it would indicate where the unwanted reflections or "flare spots" were coming from. The design would then be refined, by changing the number, size and angle of the facets, and run through the computer again. By the time the engineers reached the point of building a highly accurate model for tests on the RCS range, they would be confident that results would be close to their predictions.

At one point, Lockheed engineers were testing such a model on an outdoor RCS range east of Palmdale. At first, they were unable to detect the model at all, but, suddenly, a powerful return "bloomed" on the scope. Puzzled, the engineers looked at the target; a small bird was perching on it.

With faceting and computer modeling techniques in hand, Lockheed started to design an operational Stealth combat aircraft, virtually undetectable either by radar or by infra-red means, and capable of carrying a useful weapon load—a pair of accurate 2,000-pound bombs—over a useful range. Stealth would be achieved by the rigorous use of faceting and the best RAM that Lockheed's laboratories could develop. The rough outlines were in place by early 1976.

Have Blue

Nobody, at that point, would have dared to ask the US Air Force to provide the money to develop such an aircraft and all its subsystems, and to put it into production and service. No faceted aircraft had flown outside the wind tunnel; since the mid-1800s, no serious aircraft designer had proposed an aircraft without curvature, or camber, on its wings and tail. Also, while Lockheed had proposed ways of making a real aircraft with access doors, air inlets, control surfaces and a canopy disappear from the radar screens, the principle had been demonstrated only on a model.

Instead, Lockheed outlined a "technology demonstration" program which would prove, at the lowest possible cost, that its proposed Stealth fighter would fly properly and would indeed be virtually invisible to most radar systems. The Skunk Works would build two prototype Stealth aircraft, similar in shape to the projected fighter, but only sixty percent as large in linear dimensions. Because an aircraft's drag and lift tend to be proportional to its surface area, and its mass is proportional to its volume, they would weigh about one-third as much as the final aircraft, about 12,000 pounds fully loaded. To save money, many parts would be bought off-the-shelf: the landing gear would be that of an F-5 fighter, the Lear Siegler fly-by-wire flight control system would be the same as that of the F-16, and the General Electric J85 engines would be the same as those used on the F-5 and the Cessna A-37B light attack aircraft. Design and construction of the two prototypes would cost only $35 million.

Funding

During 1976, Ben Rich persuaded the Defense Advanced Research Projects Agency (DARPA) to fund the demonstrator program. Founded in the late 1950s as the Advanced Research Projects Agency, DARPA is tasked with supporting technology which has a relatively high risk, but a high potential payoff, and which may have multi-service applications. DARPA issued a contract to Lockheed in January 1977, and the project received the codename *Have Blue*. (Such names rarely have any literal meaning and appear to be created at random, from approved lists of words.)

President Jimmy Carter had just taken office as *Have Blue* got under way, and the potential of the program attracted the attention of his newly appointed defense under-secretary for research and engineering, William J. Perry. Together with his boss, Defense Secretary Harold Brown, Perry saw Stealth as a promising approach to many requirements and, at the same time, became nervous about entrusting its security to a largely civilian-staffed organization. DARPA was simply not equipped to handle the level of security that the project was deemed to require. During 1977, *Have Blue* was transferred to the direct control of US Air Force Systems Command, a project office was established in one of the secure vaults at the headquarters of the Aeronautical Systems Division at Wright-Patterson AFB, and the project was placed under Special Access rules.

At Burbank, construction of the two *Have Blue* aircraft proceeded rapidly. They were hand-built on quickly adjustable fixtures, just as the XP–80 and the U–2 had been; as pieces were designed, the drawings were passed down to the shop and the parts were fabricated. The plan was to demonstrate basic flying qualities on the first aircraft, and to use the second to demonstrate most of the LO (low-observables) qualities. Lockheed's Bill Park and USAF test pilot Lt. Col. Ken Dyson were to fly the aircraft.

Flight testing

Just before Christmas in 1977, with the first aircraft nearly complete, Lockheed's workforce struck over a contract dispute. Supervisors and managers were drafted as mechanics, and the aircraft was completed, apart from the attachment of its wings and tail, and was transported up to Groom Lake, where assembly was completed and the first flight took place, in January or February 1978.

The shape of the *Have Blue* prototypes is still classified. However, they generally resembled the later, full-size F–117 except that the twin rudders were located outboard of the exhausts and angled inward rather than outward. The trailing-edge shape was less deeply notched. There was no weapon bay, and the nose probes were absent, because the problem of designing a Stealthy system for airspeed measurement had not been solved. The prototypes had a conventional pitot tube, which was retracted when they were tested against radars. The inertial navigation system provided enough speed data for test purposes when the probe was retracted.

The second aircraft joined the test program in March or April. By the beginning of May, Park and Dyson had covered much of the *Have Blue* flight envelope, and the first aircraft had made few flights against radars on the Nellis range. However, the data from these tests was of limited use, because the first aircraft was not intended for RCS tests and its builders had therefore taken less time to ensure that gaps and joints were tight and sealed. Generally, the tests had gone well. Although a tendency for the aircraft to sink too fast on final approach had been discovered, it would be corrected in the production aircraft.

On May 4, 1978, Park was landing after a routine test in the first prototype when the high-sink-rate problem struck. The *Have Blue* aircraft hit the ground hard, jamming the right main landing gear in a semi-retracted position so that neither a belly landing nor a normal landing was possible. Three times, Park brought the aircraft down hard on its left main gear, trying to shake the right leg loose. It did not work, and Park was told to take the aircraft to 10,000 feet, burn off fuel and eject. The force of the ejection knocked Park's head against the headrest; although his parachute opened, he was unconscious when he hit the ground. The aircraft tumbled out of control into the Nevada desert. Park survived but never flew again. He retired as Lockheed's director of flight operations in September 1989.

RCS testing

The second aircraft was grounded at the time of the accident. Engineers were retouching its external coat of radar absorbent material (RAM) and checking the fit of doors and access panels, in preparation for tests in which the little aircraft would be flown against the entire range of Soviet radars. Located at various sites on the Nellis range, some of these had been captured by Israel in 1967 or 1973 and transferred to the United States in exchange for US military aid. Others were functional copies of Soviet radars, built by Hughes or other companies or modified from US equipment. They included the advanced microwave-frequency monopulse SA–6 tracking radar, known to the West as Straight Flush, and early-warning radars such as Bar Lock (used with most missile types) and low-frequency early warning radars such as Spoon Rest. All the radars were linked or "netted" together, as in a real Soviet-built air defense system. Airborne radars were also used in the tests, US fighter and early-warning radars being used as substitutes for advanced Soviet systems.

From mid–1978 until early 1980, Ken Dyson flew more than sixty-five sorties in the second aircraft, many of them against threat radars. The importance of detail to RCS reduction became very apparent. Doors and access panels were sealed before each series of flights with a metallic tape which compensated for differences in conductivity between different parts of the skin; RAM was then applied over the gap. Paint-type RAM was available, but had to be built up, coat by coat, by hand. To cover larger areas, flexible sheets of RAM could be cut to shape and bonded to the skin. Landing gear doors had to be carefully checked and adjusted for fit between flights. Even the gaps around the canopy and the fuel-filler door had to be filled with paint-type RAM before each signature test; the last step was always waiting for the paint to dry before take-off.

The attention to detail in the design had extended to the design of fasteners for the access panels. Conventional slot-head screws "looked like a barn door" coming over the horizon, and special screws with a curious head shape and special screwdrivers were created for the program. On one series of flights, the aircraft "bloomed" on radar at a much greater range than it ever had done before. An inspection after landing revealed that three screws were not quite tight and were fractionally extended from the skin. They were retightened and the test was repeated, successfully this time.

The results shook the skeptics. The *Have Blue* aircraft was essentially undetectable by any airborne radar except the E–3 AWACS, which was effective only at a very short range. Most ground-based missile-tracking radars would not detect it until it was inside the minimum range of the missile systems with which they were associated. Dyson's best tactic to avoid radar detection was to bore directly in on the radar, presenting the *Have Blue*'s minuscule nose-on signature. VHF radars, against which most forms of RAM are relatively ineffective, were limited to half their normal detection range. This was expected, but it was considered that these radars, such as Spoon Rest and the massive, fixed Tall King, were so large, clumsy and few in number that they could be bypassed.

Senior Trend

With these results in hand, William Perry urged the USAF to apply Stealth technology to its operational problems. In 1980, defense secretary Harold Brown was able to state that the Carter Administration had increased the rate of spending on Stealth by a factor of 100. Much of this increase would go to one program: the development and production of the full-size, operational Lockheed Stealth strike aircraft. Not surprisingly, this was a Special Access program, and it was given the codename *Senior Trend*.

Senior Trend was given the go-ahead in November 1978, on the basis of the first results of signature tests over Nevada. The USAF's operational requirement was greatly affected by the timing. Five years earlier, the Arab-Israeli war of 1973 had triggered the first use of the "oil weapon" by the Arab states that formed the Organization of Petroleum Exporting Countries (OPEC). It was a heavy blow to the West, both economically and politically. Lines at gas stations, inflation and recession had followed the OPEC action. The embargo concentrated military and political minds on the strategic situation in the Middle East.

It was not very promising. Most of the Middle Eastern countries were basically pro-Western, because the West could afford the post–1973 oil prices that were making them rich. Relationships among them, however, were edgy at best. Many of them were run by small ruling castes whose Westernized lifestyles were envied by the lower classes and despised by fundamentalists. A further uncomfortable fact was that the Soviet Union was next door to the Middle East and nervous about its own Islamic minority. Scenarios in which revolutionaries took power in one or more Middle Eastern countries, and promptly called for assistance from the Soviet Union, began to loom large. Paul Erdman's novel *The Crash of '79* was only one of a number of scenarios—published, unpublished, and classified—in which the Middle East became the world's tinder box.

The "smokeless gun"

In the event of trouble, would the Middle Eastern nations ask for help in time? And, given the great distances which any Western force would have to cover to get there, would it do any good? Questions like these, combined with the political hypersensitivity surrounding almost any foreign military involvement in the Middle East, led planners to place more emphasis on special operations forces (SOF).

Special operations defy tidy classification. They are usually located on the far side of the forward edge of the battle area (FEBA) or in an area where the FEBA is not well defined. They involve small, lightly equipped attacking forces. SOFs use concealment and covert infiltration to achieve surprise and to control the time and place of action. SOFs attack anything which does not require the heavy firepower of regular forces to destroy it and which is particularly valuable to the enemy at that particular time. SOF activities can range from the sabotage of major military installations, to hostage rescues or counter-insurgency operations.

Most SOFs, such as the Navy's SEALs or the Army's Special Forces, fight on land, whether they move by land, by air or by boat. SOF-type air operations are rare, but the assassination of Admiral Isoroku Yamamoto by the USAAF in April 1943 was an early example, as were the raids carried out by RAF Mosquito fighter-bombers against Gestapo-occupied buildings in Europe. But such operations have always been the excep-

tion rather than the rule. It is difficult to achieve surprise, because conventional aircraft are impossible to conceal in the air. Once the element of surprise is lost, a large number of support aircraft are required. And once large numbers of aircraft are involved, the active support of a neighboring government becomes essential.

A Stealth aircraft, it was realized, would be different. It would require no escort or other support aircraft, so it could be deployed discreetly without a surge of aircraft movements. If it could approach and attack its target undetected, the chances that it would be intercepted successfully would be minimal. Indeed, there would be no evidence that US aircraft had been in the region at all. Stealth might prove to be a "smokeless gun."

Special operations were a good match for the Stealth concept in other ways. Radar was still incompatible with Stealth (that would change later), and the aircraft was not invisible in daylight, so targets would be found and identified at night by infra-red sensors. These cannot see through clouds and work best in dry air, but their advantage is high resolution, which allows the target to be positively identified before weapon release. Also, a Stealth aircraft would not carry as many bombs as an F-16 or an F-4. But, in special operations, it is often important to hit the target while causing as little "collateral damage" to its surroundings as possible.

The *Senior Trend* aircraft came to be defined as a single-seat night strike fighter, with no radar but a very comprehensive electro-optical system for aiming its weapons. Because it was intended to operate at night, and had no radar, there was no requirement for any air-to-air capability. Apart from its low-observable design, its most unusual feature was associated with its covert mission: the outer wings were removable, allowing the aircraft to be stowed inside a C-5 transport. The C-5 would ferry the fighter and its support crew into a base within striking range of its target. (U-2s had used bases in Pakistan and India on similar "launch-and-leave" missions; the host governments were prepared to accept the operations as long as they were discreet.)

The USAF saw *Senior Trend* as an aircraft which would be used singly or in pairs against a small range of targets. Not many would be needed. The initial order (including five aircraft which would be used for most of the testing) consisted of around twenty aircraft, or a full squadron.

Early in 1980, before the first *Senior Trend* aircraft was in the production jigs, Ken Dyson took the second *Have Blue* prototype out of Groom Lake for some tests against the US Air Force's best fighter radar, on an F-15. Above the northern part of the Nellis range, a fuel line broke close to one of the engines, and fire broke out. Dyson tried to get the aircraft back toward Groom Lake, but the fire burned through two hydraulic lines and the controls stopped responding to the computers. Dyson ejected and the prototype fell to earth close to the Tonopah Test Range, an area mainly used for checking the drop characteristics of nuclear weapons. The pillar of smoke attracted the attention of some workers at Tonopah, who boarded trucks and raced for the crash site.

The F-15 pilot knew that the Tonopah people had no need whatsoever to see the wreckage of the top-secret aircraft. He took the imposing fighter down on the deck and motored toward the incoming trucks at 600 knots. One of them went clean off the road as the Eagle went by, and the drivers took the hint: whatever had crashed in the desert was not something that they needed to know about. They turned back to Tonopah as the helicopter from Groom Lake arrived to collect Dyson.

Political parcel bomb

A few months later, in August 1980, the Stealth story broke into the national press. There had been no leakage of information about *Senior Trend*, but there had been a clear, but unfathomable change in the US Administration's attitude toward bombers since President Carter's decision to cancel the B-1, in June 1977. The hidden factor was Stealth, which had radically increased the attractiveness of the penetrating bomber. When, in mid-1980, Congress mandated that studies of a new bomber should be started, with the aim of getting aircraft on the flight-line by 1987, the Administration briefed selected members on the US Air Force's Advanced Technology Bomber (ATB) project. By that time, several companies, including Lockheed, Rockwell, Boeing and Northrop, were competing to design the ATB, a Stealth strategic bomber.

The existence of the Stealth bomber study was reported in *Aviation Week* and the *Washington Post* in the second week of August. Carter and Brown evaluated three possible responses to the flurry of leaks and rumors. A simple "no comment" would have spurred further investigation and possible widening of the security breach. Disinformation—deliberately discrediting the reports,

Published for the first time, this photo shows the Groom Lake complex around the time of the Have Blue *program. The camera is looking west, toward the mountains which loom over the lake bed. On the left (south), just to the north of the fuel farm, are the hangars which comprise Lockheed's facility. In front of one of the three large hangars at the north end of the Groom facility is a MiG–21. The large dish antenna visible to the right was installed to measure the RCS of airborne targets. via James C. Goodall*

even though they were essentially accurate—was rejected. Instead, Carter and Brown chose to throw the wolves a bone by disclosing the existence of the *Have Blue* project, without identifying it by name. It was revealed that the program had been funded by DARPA and the USAF, and that two accidents had occurred but were unrelated to the aircraft's design. No mention was made of the rapidly progressing work on the production Stealth fighter. The facts, however, were promptly lost in a storm of criticism led by Republican candidate Ronald Reagan, who accused Carter and Brown of compromising national security for political ends.

One long-term effect of the dog-days' war over Stealth was that the existence of the Stealth fighter became a politically charged issue. President Reagan came to office in 1981, knowing that *Senior Trend* was a parcel bomb: anyone who tried to unwrap it risked having it explode in his face.

Senior Trend remained effectively classified for several more years. In October 1981, *Aviation Week* reported the development of an operational Stealth fighter, correctly noting that the initial production lot was twenty "special mission aircraft," to be in the inventory within two years, that the program was to receive $1 billion in FY1983, and that the demonstrator program had been known as *Have Blue*. The report described the aircraft as "approximately the same size as the F/A–18" and said

that it would fly "this year." The last was the only error in the piece, because the first full-scale development (FSD) aircraft in the *Senior Trend* program had already flown.

Groom Lake

Lockheed test pilot Harold (Hal) Farley had taken the first full-size Stealth fighter (USAF serial 80–780) aloft from Groom Lake on June 18, 1981. The four remaining FSD aircraft were all airborne by early 1982, and the testing task was well under way. The aircraft were delivered from Burbank to Groom Lake, with their wings removed, by C–5 transports. The flights usually took place at night. The third and fourth aircraft carried Lockheed's trademark skunk emblem on their tails. The fifth

was emblazoned with a color drawing of Elliott, the dragon from the Disney hit *Pete's Dragon*, in tribute to Col. Pete Winter, the USAF site commander at Groom Lake. (Elliott, younger readers may remember, was invisible to everyone except Pete.)

Groom Lake was busy by this time: not quite a "black Edwards," but active nevertheless. As well as five F–117s, Groom housed the secret Red Hat squadron of Mikoyan-Gurevich MiG–21s, MiG–23s and other Soviet aircraft, and a Northrop Stealth prototype—a demonstrator for the "seamless" design philosophy that Northrop used on the B–2. The Skunk Works team nicknamed it Shamu, because it resembled the famous orca at San Diego's Sea World. For a time, the Northrop or Lockheed people had to remain indoors whenever the other team's aircraft was outside, but this grew irksome; finally, the members of each team were at least cleared to set their eyes on the other's aircraft.

Security was still a concern. Ground crews were fully briefed on the projected overflight times of all known reconnaissance satellites, and of any satellites which were not yet classified; the aircraft were to be kept under cover at those times. This was also the heyday of the Red Flag exercises at Nellis, and US and allied pilots were there in hundreds, primed with rumors about goings-on at Groom. But any pilot who started to close on an F-117A got an immediate, uncompromising warning: move away or be forced down. Anyone getting within visual range of the base ran the risk of being forced down by the waiting security aircraft. The debriefing at Groom was not a pleasant experience. "We'd scare the hell out of them and send them on their way," one veteran recalls. "We would give them an intensive briefing, and tell them exactly what would happen if anything leaked."

F-117A

The Groom Lake crew called the new fighter the Scorpion, because of its menacing aspect, black finish and forked tail, but its official designation was F-117A. The designation was out of sequence. The USAF's letter-number designation system had reached F-111 by October 1962, when the Department of Defense imposed a new, cross-service system and started at F-1 again. The logical designation for the *Senior Trend* aircraft would have been F-19.

The actual designation was apparently imposed by coincidence. USAF pilots flying classified aircraft such as *Have Blue*, the MiG fighters which were also based at Groom Lake, or other prototypes were still required to log their flying hours with the USAF's central record-keeping system. For some reason lost in the mists of time and security, the code "117" was used in place of the normal aircraft designation. This number started to be used on Lockheed documents referring to the as-yet-undesignated aircraft, and the USAF decided to adopt it rather than allot a new number. The F-117A designation did not replace the *Senior Trend* codename, which continues to cover the entire operational and maintenance program.

"F-19"

In 1982, Northrop's F-5G Tigershark fighter was redesignated F-20, leading to immediate speculation that the Stealth fighter was the F-19. In fact, the USAF had skipped the number 19, because Northrop badly wanted the Tigershark to be perceived as the first of a new generation. The F-19 myth, however, proved very useful to the USAF, because the service could flatly and truthfully deny that the F-19 existed.

Test program

The test program was more comprehensive than *Have Blue*, in which it had sufficed to prove that the aircraft would fly and evade radar detection. The FSD F-117s had to generate precise performance and handling data at every point in the flight envelope. One aircraft would have been packed with strain gauges and meters to ensure that the loads on the structure in flight matched predictions. Another was probably used for most of the signature testing against the "Soviet" air defense systems at Nellis.

Every mode of the avionics system had to be tested, from normal flight to weapons delivery. Inert, guided and live weapons were launched from the internal weapons bay.

In Pentagon jargon, the F-117 program was "highly concurrent." Instead of testing the aircraft before producing it in quantity and issuing it to an operational squadron, the USAF had decided at the outset to bring the aircraft into service in the shortest possible time, allowing less than five years from the go-ahead decision to initial operational capability (IOC). Lockheed had cut metal on nearly all of the initial batch of aircraft before the F-117 made its first flight, the USAF was interviewing and selecting pilots for the program in 1980, and pilot and maintenance training was under way as soon as there were aircraft to work on.

Concurrency can be expensive if problems emerge during test flights and result in major modifications to dozens of complete and near-complete aircraft. The F-117, however, generally went well. The toughest problem appears to have been the design of the flat afterbody, the so-called "platypus." The heat of the exhaust caused the platypus to deform, losing its precisely faceted shape. Finally, a Lockheed structures expert, Henry Combs, redesigned the platypus with a "shingled" structure, which accommodated thermal expansion by allowing the panels to slide over one another.

Testing mishaps

There was only one major mishap in the test program. Early in April 1982, the first production F-117A, carrying the USAF serial 80-785, was delivered by C-5 to Groom Lake, where its wings were reinstalled and it was prepared for its first flight. Preparations were completed on April 20. Bob Ridenauer of Lockheed was to fly the aircraft. The F-117 and all its controls checked out normally on the ground. Ridenauer opened the throttles and released the brakes. The aircraft accelerated toward lift-off speed, and Ridenauer pulled back on the stick to raise the nose and take off. The instant the nosewheel left the runway, the F-117 went berserk, first yawing violently to one side and then pitching upward, out of control, while continuing to diverge in yaw. Ridenauer never had a chance to eject before the F-117 hit the runway, inverted and going backward, and caught fire.

Fortunately, the cockpit section held together and the crash trucks were on the scene in seconds. Once the fire was confirmed to be out, the crash crew cut Ridenauer out of the aircraft. He survived but was seriously injured. The remains of 80-785 ended up at Burbank as an auxiliary mock-up, used to test the fit of new components.

Investigators found that the flight control system in 80-785 had been assembled wrongly—due in part to a major design change. The gyros that measured the pitch and yaw angle were working properly, but their inputs to the flight control computer were transposed so that the computer was reading the pitch angle as yaw, and vice versa. When the aircraft pitched upward on take-off, the change in angle was detected by the gyro and fed to the yaw channel of the computer. The computer instantly compared this with Ridenauer's movements of the rudder pedals, determined that the aircraft was making an uncommanded yaw movement and "corrected" it with a hefty swing of the all-moving rudders. This caused the aircraft to make a real yaw movement, opposite to the false one detected by the computer. This movement, of course, was detected by the yaw gyro, which was connected to the pitch channel of the computer. The computer, of course, interpreted the signal as an uncommanded pitch movement and moved the elevons to correct it. Not surprisingly, the F-117 rapidly went out of control. Oddly enough, an A-12 had crashed at Groom in almost exactly similar circumstances in December 1967.

This was a high-tech version of the "crossed controls" to which older aircraft, with cable-operated controls, were vulnerable. Ridenauer had doubtless moved the controls and checked their operation before flight. But as long as the aircraft was not moving, the crossed gyros would not detect any movement, and the computer would operate the controls properly. It required real-world inputs—the movement of the whole aircraft—before the problem would surface.

Another F-117 prototype was conducting high-speed tests when one rudder separated from the aircraft. The pilot was unaware of what had happened until the pilot of the chase plane told him; that F-117 landed safely.

By mid-1982, only a year after the first flight, the F-117 was being flown not only by USAF and Lockheed test pilots, but by USAF pilots destined for the service's most secret unit: the newly formed 4450th Tactical Group. It was an elite force, because its task was to get ready to go to war in one of the most unusual aircraft of all time.

Chapter 2

Anatomy of a night predator

"If you saw it on the production line, with the wings off, you could tell it was some kind of a vehicle, and you could tell which way it was supposed to go, but you wouldn't be sure it was an airplane."

A first encounter with the F–117

Its own mother would have a hard time calling the F-117A pretty. Its external appearance is an affront to the aesthetic sense of anyone familiar with the sinuous grace of modern fighters. The F-117 is hump-backed and thick-waisted where most aircraft are sleek and tapered, and it is made up of geometrically flat panels rather than smoothly curved surfaces. Its sharply swept wings and tail imply high speed but clash with its body shape, which emphatically does not imply high speed.

The F-117 is big. Its length and span are about the same as the F-15's. It weighs about the same as an F-15 with air-to-air missiles and no external fuel. And, like the F-15, it stands high off the ground.

It is Stealth which makes the F-117A look so strange. Aircraft design leaders always used to be aerodynamicists; structures and propulsion people came second, and electrical engineers were some-

where in the bottom of the pile. A Stealth aircraft, however, is designed according to principles of electrical engineering. Radar generates an electromagnetic (EM) field around an aircraft, making it behave like an antenna. The Stealth designer's job is first to design a very bad antenna, and then to make it fly.

Edge management

"Faceting," by itself, does not absorb radar energy. But it eliminates curved surfaces, which tend to scatter radar energy equally over a wide arc, in favor of planes and edges, which reflect in a controlled and predictable manner.

Faceting equals Stealth because the flat facets will not reflect the radar beam toward the radar unless the beam is "normal" to the surface—that is to say, unless it makes two perfect right angles to the surface. The facets are aligned so that this is unlikely to happen at all. If it

31

The most striking external feature of the real F–117A is that its surface comprises flat plates, or "facets." Each facet is made sepa- *rately and attached to a skeletal aluminum substructure.* USAF photo by Eric Schulzinger of Lockheed

does, the effect will be transitory, because the aircraft is constantly moving relative to the radar and the angle of incidence is constantly changing, and no two facets will ever reflect the same beam at the same time. The edges where these surfaces meet must be perfect enough to be invisible to radar. They must be accurate to within a ten-thousandth of an inch, or they will cause untoward reflections.

Faceting is a rigorous discipline and extends to the upper and lower surfaces of the wings and the surface of the tail. But the leading and trailing edges of the wing and tail present different problems. The logic of faceting requires that intersection of two flat surfaces be infinitely sharp. Structural and aerodynamic laws dictate that the edges of the aircraft will have a measurable curved radius, resulting in reflection from the edge. Because radar echoes are gener-

ated whenever there is a break in the EM field around the aircraft, reflections will not just be created at the edges which are aligned toward the radar but also on the other side of the aircraft, and at any gap in the structure.

Edge reflections cannot be eliminated, so they are managed according to three principles. The first is to angle all the edges as sharply as possible away from the most likely and most tactically important illumination angle; that is, from about the same level and predominantly infront of the aircraft. This is why the F-117's wings are sweptback sixty-seven degrees. If a radar illuminates the edges of the aircraft from dead ahead, its main energy beam will be reflected through forty-five degrees left and right, into the sky behind the aircraft. There is no other reason for the subsonic F-117A to have such a sharply swept wing.

The second principle of edge management is to avoid inside corners, which distort the EM field along the edges. Designing a workable aircraft planform without inside corners is practically impossible, so the solution—visible on the B-2 and the F-117A—is to limit their number and put them on the back of the aircraft, where they are tactically less important. The most important edges, in the front, are ruler-straight from nose to wingtip.

The third principle of edge management is to align all edges along the smallest possible number of vectors—on a perfect design the edges would all be parallel. Edge reflections, like surface reflections, are strongest when the radar beam is at right angles to the edge. Also, radar detection range is determined by the strongest reflection, not by the total of large and small reflections. A small reflection—from an access door, for example—can be concealed under a larger one on the same bearing, if the edge of the access door is parallel to the larger edge. The reflection from the access door has, effectively, been eliminated.

A careful look at the F-117A reveals that, in plan view, the leading edges of the wings and rudders, on each side, are parallel. Each cut-off wingtip is parallel with the platypus trailing edge on the same side and with the wing trailing edge on the other side, and so on.

Other design concerns

The other dominant feature of the F-117A's shape is its wide, blended body. This is a result of a number of design concerns related to Stealth. One is the need to place the engines behind relatively deep, absorber-lined inlets and to provide them with special nozzles; an-

other is the strict need to eliminate external fuel tanks and weapon stations.

The latter is a particularly severe requirement for a tactical aircraft. Since World War II, when fighters started carrying drop tanks, the fighter designer has had the ability to change the volume and drag of the airplane in flight. On an F-16, for example, external fuel and weapons can account for more than half the take-off weight. As weapons are

The planform of the F-117A comprises a minimum number of straight lines. Not so obviously, these lines are grouped along a few primary alignments. Note, for example, that the "platypus" tail and the oblique part of the wingtip are parallel to the wing trailing edge on the opposite side, and that the edges of the landing gear doors are on the same alignments. Tony Landis

released and fuel tanks are emptied and dropped, the aircraft's weight and volume decline in proportion, and its drag decreases even more. If weapons are carried internally and external fuel tanks are taboo, the aircraft needs more usable volume. One way to provide it without a proportional increase in structural weight and surface area is by blending the wing into the body. The other distinctive feature of the F-117 body is its nearly flat underside, which will produce no strong reflections unless the radar is vertically below the fighter; and most radars cannot elevate to ninety degrees anyway.

Another principle of Stealth design is the avoidance of vertical surfaces. Tilting all surfaces at least thirty degrees away from the vertical ensures that main-lobe reflections bounce upward or downward, above the radar, unless the illuminating radar's elevation is thirty degrees above or below the aircraft. This may happen in the case of a look-down radar, but only at extremely close range. This requirement drives the designer toward a flared or chined shape, at least. A blended configuration satisfies the same conditions, its advantage being that the volume in a blended shape is more usable than the fairly narrow spaces inside the chines.

Faceting and aerodynamics

Aerodynamically, the F-117A appears to work better than one might expect. The British pioneer Sir George Cayley determined in the 1840s that a curved or cambered airfoil section was more efficient than the kite-derived flat wings which he and other inventors had used before him. Since then, lift, streamlining and curves have gone together, and it has been virtually taboo to put a sharp break in the surface profile of an airplane, except where it is parallel to the airflow. But the F-117A's body is full of such edges. Worse, even the upper surface of the wing is composed of flat

The F-117A's facets are angled at least 30 degrees away from the vertical. The broad body, which probably contributes significantly to lift, allows this shaping rule to be followed while accommodating the engines, cockpit and weapon load. The upper infrared sensor and the suck-in door above the inlet are visible. USAF photo by Eric Schulzinger of Lockheed

The F–117A was first displayed to the public on 21 April 1990 at Nellis AFB, Nevada. This

F–117A pulls away after a touch and go. James C. Goodall

facets. One Skunk Works engineer summed up the usual reaction: "My God, you're crazy."

The fact is that curvature is not a law of nature, but a design convention. An airfoil can be formed from flat surfaces as well as from curves, as long as it induces the air over its upper surface to accelerate and diminish in local pressure. A sharp break angle is likely to cause some "separation" of the airflow and an overall loss of lift and increase in drag. The question is how much separation is caused by what break angle. In the case of the F–117A, it seems that the maximum angle between two adjacent surfaces, measured streamwise, is only a few degrees.

The aerodynamics of the F-117A are similar to those of a delta-winged aircraft, like the Dassault Mirage or the Convair F-106, although the F-117A planform has been modified by the addition of a notch in the trailing edge. Deltas have a classic set of advantages and disadvantages. Deltas offer plenty of internal volume, low drag at high speed, benign handling at high angles of attack and structural simplicity. On the negative side, low speed in deltas is associated with high angles of attack and high drag; even a sophisticated delta loses speed quickly in a hard turn. On the F-117A, where maneuvering capability was of secondary importance, the designers could live with the negatives.

The F-117A may also benefit from a favorable phenomenon associated with highly swept wings: at high angles of attack, strong and stable vortices form

To save wear on the carbon-fiber brakes, the breaking parachute is used on every landing. James C. Goodall

The parachute is all-black and emerges from a bay that is just forward of the V-tail. James C. Goodall

above the leading edge, and have the effect of keeping the airflow over the rest of the wing attached and stable. This may explain why the F-117A's low-speed behavior and its landing performance appear better than one might expect of a heavy aircraft with a sharply swept wing. Nevertheless, the aircraft lifts off and lands at a relatively high speed: lift-off occurs around 180 knots, and the final approach is flown at 150 knots.

Controls

The F-117A's controls are conventional. Each wing carries two elevons,

An F-117A is shown taxiing in front of two of the other aircraft types in the Air Force's ground attack arsenal: F-15Es from Luke *AFB, Arizona, and A-10s from England AFB, Louisiana.* James C. Goodall

Crew members of the 37th TFW perform the post-flight inspection on the F-117As. James C. Goodall

The pickup truck parked near this F–117A gives an indication of how large the F–117A is. James C. Goodall

which control the aircraft in pitch and roll. The hinge lines are apparently sealed by flexible RAM panels, to maintain low reflectivity as the surfaces move. The dramatically swept V-tail provides directional stability and control. Unlike most V-tails, it has no pitch-control function. Structurally, the tails resemble those of the SR–71, with a fixed stub and an all-moving rudder which pivots around a

fixed shaft that runs along its aerodynamic centerline. The hinge-line, however, is Z-shaped, in accordance with the principles of edge management. The fixed and moving surfaces are faceted at the hinge-line to further reduce reflection.

Like most fighters since the F–16, the F–117 is not naturally stable; neither was *Have Blue.* A naturally stable Stealth

The F–117As are directed to the display area. James C. Goodall

aircraft could probably have been built, but it would have needed a larger, heavier tail and would have been less efficient and less maneuverable. The F-117A has an analog flight control system (FCS) developed by Lear Siegler Astronics (now GEC Astronics), which provides the necessary stability by artificial means. The aircraft's attitude and flight-path are monitored by a system of gyroscopes and accelerometers, and any deviations are sensed and corrected by small control movements. This process takes place as much as forty times a second, so the deviations are not perceived to the pilot.

The only way to make an aircraft's hydraulically powered control surfaces respond so fast is to use electronic signals, rather than mechanical rods or cables, to open and close the valves on the rams which move the controls. This is why the F-117's control system (and others like it) is described as "fly-by-wire" (FBW).

Without its computer-based controls, the F-117A is unflyable. What makes it safe is that the system is quad-

The F-117A's cockpit is wide and roomy, compared to other modern single-place aircraft. The canopy is raised by two hydraulic rams, one on each side of the all-black ACES II ejection seat. Note the wide control panel, HUD and the pilot's all-black helmet. James C. Goodall

redundant, having four independent channels all controlling the same functions, and the system constantly compares their signals. If one signal differs from the others it is assumed to have failed, and is shut down. (Normally, the pilot would land as soon as possible after such a failure.) The system still has three channels, so that a second failure can be detected, located and isolated on the same principle. A third failure would present problems, but is extremely unlikely.

A great deal of simulation and test work went into the refinement of the FCS, because the way in which the aircraft responds to the pilot, or to outside

The pilot looks out through five flat glass panels. Visibility is good forward and to the sides, but is poor downward and upward and blind to the rear. James C. Goodall

The pilot enters and leaves the cockpit via an external ladder. Note the leading edge protector. James C. Goodall

disturbances, depends on the FCS computer.

Stealth has one direct effect on flight control system design. The FCS needs to know at all times how fast the aircraft is moving through the air and at what angle. Normally, this information is provided through a pitot probe, which measures speed, and small vanes, resembling weathercocks, which monitor the direction of the airflow over the body, but they cannot be designed with low RCS. Instead, four air-pressure probes, of diamond section with pyramid-like tips, are located on the leading edge of the aircraft. The tip of each probe has five holes, one in the center of the tip and one in the center of each tip facet. Differential readings from the holes provide the FCS with information on speed, angle of attack and yaw angle. Each probe connects to an FCS channel. Retractable backup probes (of conventional design) are also installed.

Airframe materials

The F-117 is mostly made of aluminum alloy, probably with some titanium around the engines and exhaust system. When *Senior Trend* was given the go-ahead in 1978, the most extensive use of non-metallic composites on a production fighter was on the just-completed F/A-18, which had graphite/epoxy wing skins attached to metal spars and ribs. For Senior Trend, which already pushed the state of the art in many ways, the choice of metal was not surprising; one

This photo shows the location of the HUD controls. Moveable cockpit lights are at- *tached to the rear of the canopy rails.* James C. Goodall

of the Skunk Works' mottos is KISS—Keep It Simple, Stupid. The structure is stressed to 7g.

Faceting imposes restrictions on the way the aircraft is assembled, because no known means of forming metal can produce an edge that is precise and stable enough for faceting to work. Instead, the facets are separate and are anchored to a complex skeleton structure. While the *Have Blue* prototypes were largely hand-built, the facets being trimmed and adjusted until a perfect fit was achieved, this was not possible for the F-117A, so production tooling was designed, built and installed to toler-

ances that were roughly one-tenth of those for tooling used to build previous aircraft.

Radar-absorbent material

While the structure of the F-117 uses conventional materials, the entire exterior surface of the aircraft is covered with very special material. Radar-absorbent material (RAM) has been in existence almost as long as radar itself. Known types all work on the same basic principle.

Radar signals are electromagnetic waves and bounce efficiently off any conductive object. However, the elec-

This photo is of the port side of the fuselage, below the canopy. To the lower left of photo is the emergency canopy blow-off T-handle. The white pyramid shape above and to the right of the T-handle is the engine inlet illumination light (for performing a visual icing check while in flight). The circle of holes to the right of the ejection seat warning triangle is a static port to measure side slip. The diamond-shaped cover at upper right covers a backup (non-stealth) pitot tube. There is one inlet illumination light, one static port and one backup pitot tube on each side of the cockpit. James C. Goodall

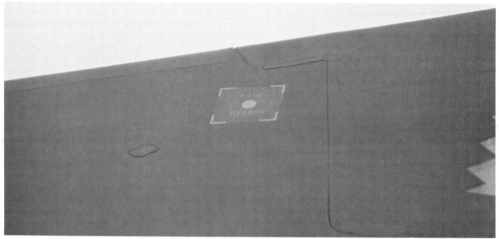

This photo shows the area to the aft of the canopy on the starboard side. The area marked "Fire, Pierce" is the emergency mechanical canopy release. To the left of the release is a retractable instrument landing system antenna. There is a canopy release and antenna on each side. James C. Goodall

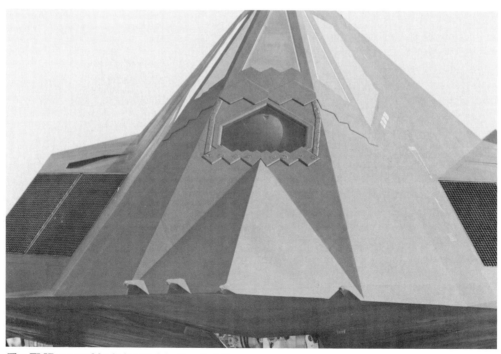

The FLIR assembly is located in front of the canopy. James C. Goodall

tromagnetic characteristics of different objects and materials are not the same. One of the best demonstrations of this principle is the domestic microwave oven. Its energy source is a powerful, crude magnetron, a radar-wave generator invented during World War II.

While some substances reflect radar waves efficiently, others do not. The difference lies in their molecular structure. Some materials, including many organic substances (such as food), include "free electrons" in their molecular chains. Electrical engineers call them "lossy." Radars, like radios and televisions, operate on a given wavelength; in the case of most radars, the wavelength is measured in gigahertz (GHz), or billions of cycles per second. When a radar transmitter illuminates an object with such characteristics, the free electrons are forced to oscillate back and forth at the frequency of the radar wave. But these particles have friction and inertia, however tiny, and the process is not 100 percent efficient; the radar's energy is transformed into heat.

Foods are "lossy dielectrics" because they are inefficient conductors. The early types of RAM developed in World War II were lossy dielectrics, mostly using carbon as the active ingredient.

Other materials, including glass, ceramics and many plastics, are simply "dielectric." They do not conduct electricity and radar waves pass straight through them with minimal reflection or absorption, even at high power levels. This is why such materials are used in microwave utensils and aircraft radomes.

Another major group is the "lossy magnetic" materials, typically iron compounds called ferrites, or carbonyl iron.

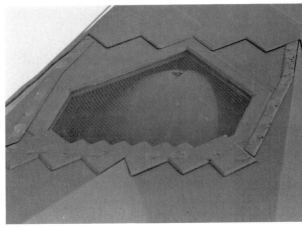

The back of the FLIR head is visible through the RAM-mesh screen that covers the seeker head bay. The FLIR head is shown in the stowed position. In flight, it is rotated through 80 degrees so that the infra-red sensors point forward. The edges of the FLIR housing are sawtoothed and faceted. Note the RAM putty that coats the fasteners. James C. Goodall

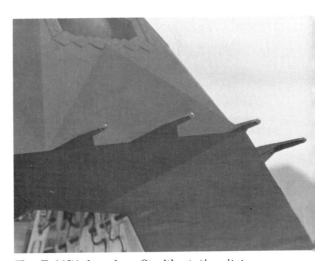

The F–117A has four Stealth static pitot tubes at the leading edge of the nose. These pitot tubes are constructed of an electrically conductive plastic, developed by Lockheed, and are heated to keep them clear of ice. James C. Goodall

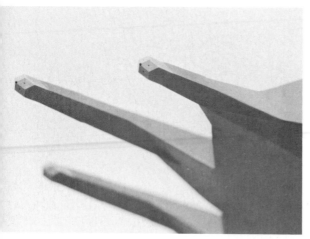

The tip of each pitot tube is pyramid shaped, with one hole in the center of the tip and one hole in the center of each tip facet. There are two more input holes on each facet of the diamond-section tubes. James C. Goodall

A radar wave induces a magnetic field in the ferrite material, but the field must switch polarity at the radar frequency. As in the case of the lossy dielectric, this process is not 100 percent efficient and much of the energy is transformed into heat.

A third class, circuit analog (CA) RAM, has been used in some applications. CA absorbers consist of conductive metal, usually deposited in a thin film on a dielectric substrate. The film is deposited in a carefully designed pattern, so that the electrical energy of the radar wave dissipates itself as it runs around and between the conductive elements.

Many forms of RAM are not even classified. Most such material consists of

The DLIR is located on the underside of the fuselage, starboard of the nose gear bay. The seeker head is identical to the FLIR's, with the addition of a boresighted laser designa- *tor. Images from the FLIR and DLIR are displayed on a 12 inch CRT in the center of the instrument panel. James C. Goodall*

an active ingredient—a dielectric, such as carbon, or magnetic ferrites—which is molded into a non-lossy dielectric matrix, usually a plastic of some kind. Lockheed developed a lossy paint for the A-12 and D-21. Goodyear (now Loral Defense Systems) has provided a material that resembles a ferrite-loaded neoprene, which is used in the inlet ducts of the B-1.

Perfect RAM does not exist. All types absorb a portion of the radar energy and reflect the rest. All known types of RAM are most effective at a certain frequency and less so at others. Similarly, the effectiveness of RAM varies with the angle of the incident radar wave. RAM can be made to perform well

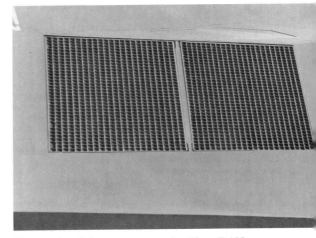

The engine inlets are covered with a RAM grid. The grid is coated with an electrically conductive paint that heats it, keeping it clear of ice. James C. Goodall

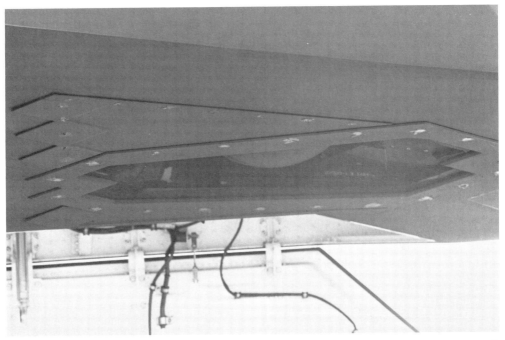

This side view of the DLIR assembly shows the RAM-mesh screen over the bay opening, the sawtoothed and faceted edges and the

RAM putty over the fasteners. James C. Goodall

Two elevons are at the trailing edge of each wing. The edges of the elevons are faceted to control reflection. James C. Goodall

The hinge lines between the wings and elevons are sealed with flexible RAM. James C. Goodall

over a broad bandwidth by using layers; the snag is that the thickness and weight of RAM increase with its effectiveness.

Generally, magnetics perform best against long-wavelength radars, such as the many older VHF and UHF radars which are in service with the Soviet armed forces, whereas dielectrics and CA are optimized at the microwave frequencies where more modern radars operate.

In the latest Stealth aircraft, such as the B–2 and the Advanced Tactical Fighter, the radar-absorbent elements are built into the primary structure. This technology, however, was not mature when the F–117A was being designed, so it uses the older non-load-bearing or "parasitic" RAM. It is believed to comprise multiple layers of magnetic RAM, and the lay-up differs on different parts of the aircraft. For instance, the forward fuselage is likely to carry more RAM than the top of the body, since it is

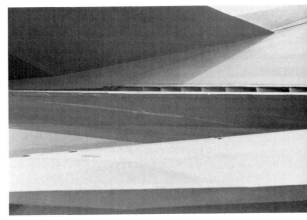

The exhaust is shielded from view below and to the rear by the upward swept platypus, reducing the chance of IR detection. James C. Goodall

more directly illuminated from a more critical angle.

At the start of the program, the RAM came in flexible sheets, rather like linoleum in thickness and texture, which

This rear view shows the long, thin exhaust duct. James C. Goodall

The moveable rudders mate to the tail stubs at a Z-shaped hinge line. James C. Goodall

were cut to the shape of each facet and were secured to the metal substructure with adhesive. They consisted of active ferrite ingredients set in a synthetic polymer matrix. Worn or weathered panels could be removed and replaced during overhaul.

The RAM was supplemented with a paint-like absorber, which was used to coat gaps between RAM panels. For an operational mission into a hostile area, RAM paint or tape would be used to seal the engine-bay doors and other access panels. Other forms of RAM are probably used to line the inlet ducts and to form radar-absorbing seals for the cockpit canopy and the doors for the landing gear and weapons bay.

This view, directly from the rear, shows more of the faceting at the hinge line and the parachute doors, just forward of the V-tail.

Note how well the platypus conceals the exhaust duct. James C. Goodall

More recently, the F–117A fleet has changed to an overall paint-type RAM. Technically, there is no reason RAM cannot be applied as a fluid; the main practical objection has been that it is extremely difficult to apply the material accurately and consistently. The solvents needed to make the RAM fluid are also hazardous to health. Apparently, the problem has been solved by the use of robotics. The Tonopah base has been provided with a new painting facility in which the aircraft is held in a rotary fixture, like a gigantic fowl on a spit, while computer-controlled nozzles spray RAM on to the aircraft in a precisely controlled pattern.

A typical conventional fighter has a head-on RCS of five square meters; that is to say, it seems as large on radar as a radar-reflective sphere with a cross-section of that size, which would be just over eight feet in diameter. From certain aspects, if parts of the structure are flat plates or act as "retro-reflectors", the RCS is much larger. The combination of shaping and RAM gives the F–117 an RCS between 0.01 square meter (a 4.5 inch sphere) and 0.001 square meter (a 1.4 inch sphere), according to radar wavelength and aspect. This is roughly equivalent to typical RCS values for small birds or insects.

In practical terms, this means that a radar which can pick up the conventional fighter reliably at eighty-five miles range will not detect the F–117 until it is sixteen miles away, at the maximum; its effective range may be as little as eight miles.

Design features

Internal details of the F–117A are influenced by the need to accommodate all components, weapons and fuel inside the low-RCS faceted envelope and the original requirement that the wings be readily removable for transport. The F–117A is built up around a box-like center section, starting immediately aft of the cockpit and extending to a point level with the wing trailing edge, which accommodates the engines, the weapon bay, the main landing gear and much of the fuel. Ahead of this box is the pyramidical cockpit, above the nosewheel bay, and the nose, which holds most of the avionics. Behind it is a wide, flat tail fairing, colloquially known as the platypus, which accommodates the engine exhaust mixer and supports the dramatically swept V-tail.

The central box is built around a number of complex transverse frames, probably machined from large one-piece forgings, which carry the main loads from the wing around the engine and weapon bays. One of these frames also carries the attachment points for the forward-retracting main landing gear. Much of the lower skin can be opened,

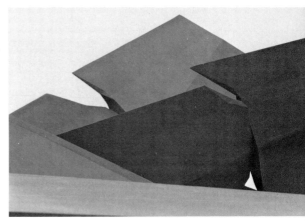

This side view of the V-tail shows more of the faceting at the hinge lines and of the rudder surfaces. James C. Goodall

49

This rear view of the fuselage shows two features that are added, for safety, to F-117As on training flights: an anticollision beacon (on top surface) and a radar reflector (the pyramid-shaped device near the US insignia) to give it a normal radar return. At the peak is a rear-facing inflight refueling receptacle light. James C. Goodall

Looking forward at the underside, this photo shows the split weapon bay doors. The doors are sawtooth edged fore and aft and hinge at the outboard edges. The faceted, diamond shaped devices cover the hinge attachment points. Outboard of the weapon bay doors are the engine bay access doors. James C. Goodall

taking into account the weapon bays, the engine access panels and the main landing gear compartments; longitudinal beams on each side of the weapon bay provide the necessary strength. The space above the weapon bays accommodates much of the 2,000 US gallon fuel load and the refueling receptacle, which opens by rotating about its longitudinal axis. Auxiliary tanks can be carried in the weapon bays for long ferry flights.

All the edges of the doors and access panels are either straight fore and aft, aligning with the wing and rudder tips, or they are aligned with the trailing edge of the platypus. The weapon-bay doors are saw-toothed at their front and rear ends. The tooth angles are aligned with each side of of the platypus.

All three landing gear legs retract forward. The gear doors are polygonal, with no right-angle corners or straight edges at right angles to the airplane's line of flight. A brake parachute is installed above the rear of the fuselage, and is used routinely to reduce wear on the brakes. Also, an arrester hook is fitted underneath the platypus and can be used in the event of brake problems. The F-117A was one of the first USAF aircraft to use carbon brake discs, which are significantly lighter and smaller than steel discs of the same capacity.

Propulsion system

The design of a Stealth aircraft's propulsion system poses its own challenges because nobody has yet built a production turbine engine that is not 100 percent metal, or created an effective absorber that would not erode away from an engine's rotating parts. Therefore, a Stealth aircraft needs an inlet and exhaust system which allows air to pass efficiently but obstructs radar waves. The exhaust must also prevent the heat of the engine exhaust from betraying the aircraft's presence to infrared sensors. This is difficult with a non-afterburning engine but impossible with an afterburner, so afterburners are taboo.

Engine

The F-117's engines are conventional. A new or highly modified engine would have been expensive and was not necessary, so Lockheed had to choose among available engines. The aircraft needed more thrust than any one available engine could provide without afterburning. Together with the consequences of an engine failure on one of the F-117's highly clandestine missions, this drove the designers toward twin engines.

Stealth had one direct influence on the choice of engine: the inlet and exhaust systems would be proportional in size, weight and complexity to the mass of air passing through the engine. Therefore, while a high-bypass-ratio turbofan engine (like the General Electric TF34) might be more efficient at the F-117A's operating speed, a lower-bypass engine would actually result in a lighter, smaller aircraft.

The Lockheed designers selected two General Electric F404 engines to power the F-117. The F404 is a very-low-bypass turbofan engine, originally developed as an afterburning fighter engine for the F/A-18. GE's original concept was a turbojet engine with a "leak" aft of the low-pressure compressor, providing just enough air to, first, cool the outer casing and, second, to feed the augmentor with enough air to attain a desired thrust increase with afterburner. Adapt-

The nose gear bay is covered by one saw-toothed, faceted door. James C. Goodall

ing the F404 for the F-117 was a relatively simple matter of removing the augmentor, the variable nozzle and the related fuel, hydraulic and control subsystems. The modified engine is designated F404-F1D2. One of its best features is its thrust/weight ratio of 6:1. This is an excellent figure for a non-afterburning engine and is actually better than the previous generation of augmented turbofans.

Inlet system

The F-117A's inlets and exhaust are as radical as any feature of the aircraft. The inlets are covered at the front with a grid of thin, knife-edged blades, spaced only an inch or so apart. The grids are faceted in cross-section and coated with absorbent material. Incoming radar signals are partly absorbed

The main gear bay is covered by two doors. Note the faceting on the outer skin of the door

and the retractable antenna, to the left of the gear. James C. Goodall

and partly reflected around the grid and into the inlet ducts, which are lined with RAM. (One *Have Blue* prototype lost an engine when a RAM sheet came loose and was swallowed by the compressor.) Any signal reaching the metal compressor face has to make its way back through the absorber-lined duct and the grid.

The inlets apparently work well at normal speeds and attitudes; as in the case of the faceted airfoil, just because something does not accord with the normal way of doing things does not mean that it is physically impossible. At low speeds or high angles of attack, the inlets cannot provide enough air to the engines and are augmented by a pair of large "suck-in" doors above the inlet ducts. If the pressure in the inlet drops, the differential between the inlet pressure and the outside pressure forces these spring-loaded doors to open inward. In normal flight, the pressure differential is in the reverse direction, keeping the doors firmly seated. However, the dorsal suck-in doors are not as efficient as the forward-facing inlets, so engine thrust and efficiency decline at high angles of attack.

The most serious single problem in the development of the inlets was satisfactory de-icing. Tactical fighters fly fast enough to avoid most icing problems; skin friction keeps the surfaces warm enough to prevent a significant build-up of ice. The slightly convergent passages formed by the F-117A inlet grid, however, act like a venturi and cause the air to accelerate, lose pressure and to cool down. Even a thin build-up of ice could swiftly choke the narrow passages, further constricting the airflow and encouraging more ice formation. The first

F-117As were under strict orders to avoid any area of suspected icing until the problem was solved. Now, a coat of electrically resistant paint is applied beneath the RAM and acts as an electrical heating element, keeping the passages open. Even so, a small light is built into the fuselage on each side of the cockpit so that the pilot can check the grids for icing at night.

It has been suggested that the high-pitched whine which can be heard from in front of an approaching F-117A is caused by multiple small wakes which are shed from the intersections of the inlet grid, propagate down the duct and strike the spinning compressor blades. As the blades "chop" these wakes, they create a high-frequency sound wave which propagates back up the duct and ahead of the aircraft.

Exhaust system

The exhaust system is designed to reduce infra-red emissions from the aircraft—or, more exactly, to reduce the detectability of those emissions—while also masking the rear of the engine from radar.

The exhaust changes shape from a circle at the back of the engine to a wide slot, several feet across but only six inches deep, that extends across the rear of the platypus. Baffles extending some eight inches into the rear of the exhaust break up radar signals, and the extreme rear edge of the aircraft, behind the exhaust slot, is covered with heat-reflecting tiles, similar in principle to the tiles used on the Space Shuttle Orbiter. Bypass air from the engine is used to cool the metal structure.

The exhaust is designed to deal with the two basic sources of detectable infra-red emission: the hot exhaust plume and metal parts of the aircraft which are heated by the exhaust. The shape of the nozzle flattens the plume, so that its perimeter is larger in relation to its area (and its mass) than it would be if it were round. This makes the plume dissipate more rapidly after it leaves the aircraft. The baffles block direct visibility of the hot engine parts, and the tiles reflect the infra-red radiation from the plume rather than absorbing it, as metal tends to do.

Visibility

The F–117A's strange forward body shape reconciles a number of conflicting requirements. The pilot needs a reasonable degree of outside visibility but, in particular, needs to see the runway on approach. The F–117A has a highly swept wing and no high-lift devices, so it approaches the runway at a nose-high angle. The pilot's eyeline must be high enough, and the nose short enough, to let him see the runway. Also, the logic of faceting and aerodynamics would tend to dictate a V-shaped windshield (as used on the SR–71), with a single edge line running from the nose to the canopy roof, but this is not acceptable for low-level night attack operations.

This view shows the inside of the landing gear assembly. James C. Goodall

This view shows the outside of the landing gear assembly. Note the landing light. James C. Goodall

The F-117A, therefore, has a small flat windshield set in a flat facet. Beneath the windshield is a sensor housing, and beneath this, a triangular "beak" juts out, streamlining the nose and continuing the leading-edge line. Two narrow facets carry small windows (resembling vent windows on a car) which provide front-quarter visibility, particularly into a turn. The largest windows are on each side of the cockpit, where they are probably least useful except for helping the pilot maintain his orientation. Forward and side visibility is adequate, but the pilot can barely see down, upward or backward at all.

The windows are treated to reduce radar reflectivity. It is possible that some kind of circuit analog RAM could be built into a laminated transparency. It is most important to prevent radar from detecting objects inside the cockpit, so the window treatment probably includes a transparent, conductive film or coating on its inner surface to block incoming radar waves.

The entire canopy, including the windshield, hinges upward from a point well aft of the seat. Larger and heavier than a conventional canopy, it is fitted with two powerful explosive rams which can open it completely in a fraction of a second when the pilot pulls the ejection handle. The ejection-seat sequencer fires the seat when a switch confirms that the canopy is clear. The seat is a special, all-black ACES II unit produced by Mc-Donnell Douglas.

The cockpit itself is unusual, because of the pyramid shape of the forward fuselage. It is very narrow at the top, leaving the pilot only a few inches of space on either side of his helmet, but unusually wide lower down.

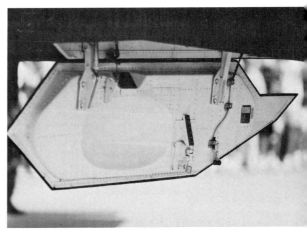

The inner surface of the landing gear bays are painted white. James C. Goodall

Navigation and attack system

Making the F-117A virtually undetectable, making it flyable, and making it able to carry a weapon load were achievements in themselves. However, a military aircraft also has to be able to find and hit its targets, and this presented more problems.

The F-117A's weapon-delivery requirements were a product, in part, of Vietnam experience. By the end of the first Rolling Thunder bombing campaigns of 1965–68, the USAF had dropped an enormous tonnage of bombs on Vietnam, and it was painfully obvious that most of them missed anything important. Even strikes against known, fixed targets were difficult. Heavy, constantly alerted defenses made the most accurate form of attack (dive-bombing from 10,000 feet) virtually suicidal, but low-level, high-speed attacks were inaccurate. In particular, two important bridges—the Paul Doumer and Than Hoa spans—survived dozens of raids and thousands of bombs.

When US bombing resumed in 1972 under Linebacker I, the Paul Doumer and Than Hoa bridges went down within days, each dropped by direct hits from new bombs which homed in on the energy from a laser beam, usually transmitted from the launch aircraft or a companion aircraft. The lesson incorporated into the F-117A was that the laser-guided weapon's accuracy counted for more than quantity.

Forward-looking infra-red

Vietnam also saw the first operational use of forward-looking infra-red (FLIR) sensors, which can produce TV-quality pictures of distant objects on clear nights. Unlike radar, infra-red sensors do not produce emissions that betray the presence of the attacker. And their higher resolution allows the pilot to pick out either small targets or individual features of large targets.

The chief limitation of FLIR, compared with radar, is that a system of practical size can "image" only a small area at the resolution needed to identify targets. Searching for targets with FLIR has been compared to looking through a soda straw; to be used effectively, it needs to be pointed in the right direction first.

Inertial navigation system

Most night-attack aircraft rely on radar and an inertial navigation system (INS) to find their targets and cue the FLIR. INS is basically an array of gyroscopes, accelerometers and computers. From the moment that the aircraft rolls away from its parking space, it adds up every acceleration, deceleration, turn, pitch and roll of the aircraft, and thus computes its current position. Its drawback is that it tends to drift, or lose accuracy, with time, but it can direct the

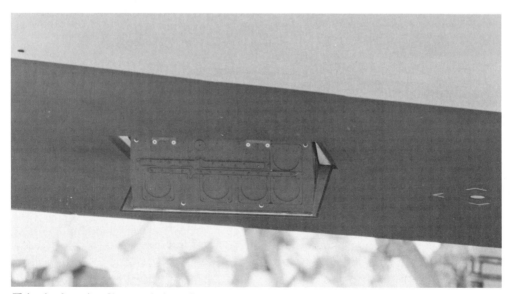

This single-point diagnostic interface panel is on the underside of the port wing, near the leading edge. James C. Goodall

aircraft to a point where the search radar can pick out the target. The radar can then "cue" the FLIR.

In the late 1970s, however, there was no acceptable radar available for the F–117A. Anything in service or under development would emit so much radiation that the fighter's presence would be obvious. "Low probability of intercept" (LPI) radar, specifically designed for Stealth aircraft, was in its embryonic stage and would not be available for service until the 1990s.

Instead, the F–117A navigation/attack system is designed around a FLIR/laser system and a very accurate INS.

Markings for the 415th TFS, 416th TFS and 37th TFW were painted on the two F–117As

displayed at Nellis. Operational aircraft are devoid of all markings. James C. Goodall

The F-117 is broad when seen from underneath and solid in front-view, but is surprisingly slender from the side. The dramatic sweep angle of the swallow-tail rud- *ders places much of their area well aft, for maximum effectiveness. USAF photo by Eric Schulzinger of Lockheed*

Developed by Honeywell, the INS uses the same technology as the systems used for the B-52 bomber and the MX missile: the gyros and other instruments are built into a metal sphere, which is suspended by a powerful magnetic field. Systems based on this "electrostatic gimbal" technology have demonstrated circular error probability growth rates of one-tenth of a nautical mile. In plain language, this means that the system is guaranteed to navigate the F-117A for 600 miles and arrive within 200 yards of its objective. Performance is often much better than that. The limitation, according to an F-117 pilot, is that target coordinates are not always as accurate as the INS.

The FLIR/laser system is unique. One FLIR is installed ahead of the windshield, behind a RAM-treated mesh screen. A second system, the downward-looking infra-red (DLIR), is mounted below the body of the aircraft. Both the FLIR and DLIR are steerable and stabilized. The FLIR has a wide field of view

The lower lip of the F-117A's exhaust inclines upward, virtually concealing it from *observation at the same level. USAF photo by Eric Schulzinger of Lockheed*

(WFOV) and a narrow field of view (NFOV) optical system. The DLIR has a boresighted laser designator.

FLIR imagery or DLIR imagery is displayed on a large cathode-ray tube (CRT) screen which dominates the instrument panel; it is the primary flight instrument and, particularly at night, is the primary focus of the pilot's attention. Airspeed, attitude and navigation information are superimposed on the FLIR view. Smaller multi-function displays (MFDs), about five inches square, are mounted on each side of the central CRT and provide the pilot with information about the status of the aircraft systems, communications and weapons.

Normally, the pilot will fly using the FLIR locked forward in its wide-field mode, which gives a natural view of the terrain on the head-up display. Close to the target, however, the INS can steer the FLIR toward the location of the target. The pilot can search for the target on the screen and can select the

"telephoto" NFOV mode for positive identification and for aiming weapons. The FLIR probably also has an automatic tracking mode, in which it locks on to the target and tracks it as the aircraft moves. Alternatively, the FLIR can be rotated 180 degrees to minimize its visibility, and the pilot can fly on instruments.

Weapons

If the mission calls for a laser-guided bomb (LGB) attack from level flight, the target will pass beneath the aircraft and disappear from the FLIR's field of view before the bombs hit. This is where the DLIR comes in. On a level run, the pilot can switch from the upper sensor unit to the lower unit, which will continue to track the target as the aircraft passes over it. The pilot "lases" the target for the last few seconds before impact, and the LGB makes the necessary corrections to ensure a direct hit. Presumably, the DLIR can also record

A line of baffles in the slit-like exhaust serves two functions. The baffles help to protect the rear of the engine from detection, and they also clamp the nozzle sides together, resisting their natural tendency to swell into a *rounded shape under pressure. Also visible in this view is one of the retractable blade aerials. USAF photo by Eric Schulzinger of Lockheed*

the target image at impact, for subsequent assessment.

The F–117A's internal weapons bay, about the same size as the F–111's, is designed to carry two weapons in the 2,000-pound class. In theory, the aircraft could carry nuclear weapons—the F–117A is nuclear-certified and carries standard nuclear arming and safing systems, like all Tactical Air Command aircraft—but there are few scenarios under which such a capability would be used. More probably, the aircraft is armed with precision-guided bombs produced by adding guidance kits to a standard warhead.

GBU–10 Paveway II

A typical laser-guided weapon is the GBU–10 Paveway II, which consists of a special nose and tail section attached to a standard 2,000 pound MK 84 bomb. The tail section incorporates folding aerodynamic surfaces which allow the bomb to glide rather than follow a standard ballistic path. The nose section includes the laser seeker, guidance electronics, and control fins. The Paveway II kit can steer the bomb on to the target, provided it does not have to perform any drastic changes in direction. It follows that the bomb will hit its target provided that it is released at a speed, distance and altitude that will place it inside the capture envelope of the guidance system. The envelope, colloquially known as "the basket," resembles an inverted cone with its point on the target. Once the bomb is inside the basket, its seeker can lock on to reflected laser energy and steer the weapon to a direct hit.

Some weapons may have been developed specifically for the F–117, but no firm information is available about them.

However, the aircraft probably carries one new weapon about which information has been released. In the early 1980s, it was realized that even 2,000 pound laser-guided weapons were remarkably ineffective against well-designed reinforced concrete structures. It might be better to say that the fact had been rediscovered; British aircraft designer Barnes Wallis had come to the same conclusion in 1940. Standard bombs, with cheap rolled-steel cases, tend to break up on contact with very hard surfaces, causing surface damage and little else. The 12,000 pound Tallboy and 22,000 pound Grand Slam bombs, which Wallis designed for use against submarine pens and missile-launching complexes, featured thick one-piece cases, filled at the tail end, smoothly tapered noses to bore through hard ground or concrete, and rugged delay fuzes.

BLU–109/B

In 1984, a new study showed that many targets in Eastern Europe and elsewhere were being protected to the point where even a direct hit with a 2,000 pound bomb would leave them dented but functional. Under the codename *Have Void*, an improved weapon was developed by Lockheed Missiles & Space Company. It was delivered to users, probably including the 4450th Tactical Group, in December 1985. It is also known as the I–2000 (Improved 2,000 pound) and as the BLU–109/B, and it is normally mated to the GBU–10 laser-guidance kit.

The BLU–109/B is a slim, bullet-shaped bomb with a tail fuze and forged case of hardened steel, made in one piece apart from the tail plug. In rocket-sled and live drop tests, BLU–109/B warheads have penetrated reinforced concrete more than six feet thick, remained intact and detonated reliably within the structure, tossing forty-ton slabs of concrete over the test range. Against softer targets, such a weapon will bury itself deeply before detonating, sending shock waves rippling through the ground and causing massive disruption.

GBU-24 Paveway III

Other laser-guided weapons include the GBU-24 Paveway III, a more modern weapon with larger tail surfaces and a more efficient navigation system which causes the bomb to follow a more efficient track to its target. Paveway III is also known as the Low Level LGB (LLLGB), because its better gliding characteristics allow it to be released at low altitude, some distance from the target.

Apart from being essentially undetectable in operation, this kind of weapon-delivery system is extremely accurate. Typically, laser-guided weapons land within feet of the point illuminated

The General Electric F404–GE–100D engine is similar to the F404–F1D2 in the F-117A. The engine was designed to be serviced or removed from beneath the aircraft; all accessories are grouped on the bottom of the engine and can be changed without removing the complete powerplant. General Electric

by the launch aircraft. They can be aimed with high confidence at any one of a cluster of small buildings, at a specific window or door of a large building, at one component of an industrial or military target, the pier of a suspension bridge, the control center of a missile site, the most critical section of a highway interchange or a railroad marshaling yard or a particular ship among

1	*Pitot head*
2	*Air-data probes*
3	*Electro-optical scanner window*
4	*Steerable IR and laser designator head*
5	*Electro-optical navigation, target acquisition and designation system module*
6	*Ventral scanner window*
7	*Nosewheel bay*
8	*Forward-retracting nose landing gear*
9	*Rudder pedals and control column*
10	*Cockpit multi-function CRT displays*
11	*Upward hinging one-piece canopy and windshield*
12	*Canopy actuators and jettison struts*
13	*ACES II ejection seat*
14	*Avionics equipment bay*
15	*Port engine air intake*
16	*Intake shielding grid*
17	*Equipment bay, hydraulics and air conditioning, port and starboard*
18	*Intake suction relief door*
19	*Forward fuselage fuel tank*
20	*Extending ILS glideslope aerials*
21	*Starboard suction relief door, open*
22	*Retractable/detachable communications aerial*
23	*Radar return augmentor*
24	*Engine bay vent*
25	*Starboard engine bay*
26	*Rotating refueling receptacle*
27	*Center fuselage fuel tank*
28	*Ventral weapons bay, two 2000 lb LGBs shown*
29	*General Electric F404–F1D2 engine*
30	*Flush aerial panel*

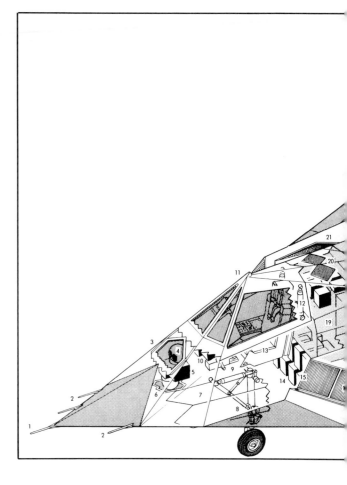

31	*Engine bay by-pass air mixing duct*
32	*Multi-lobe exhaust nozzle*
33	*Runway emergency arrestor hook stowage*
34	*Rear fuselage fuel tanks*
35	*Exhaust nozzle vanes*
36	*Fin hydraulic actuators*

many in a harbor. A laser-guided weapon can hit many small objectives with minimal collateral damage.

In April 1990, the USAF stated that the F-117A can carry "the full range of tactical munitions." Since the USAF defines a "munition" as almost anything which can be dropped from an aircraft, this implied that it could launch almost any missile in the inventory. More re-

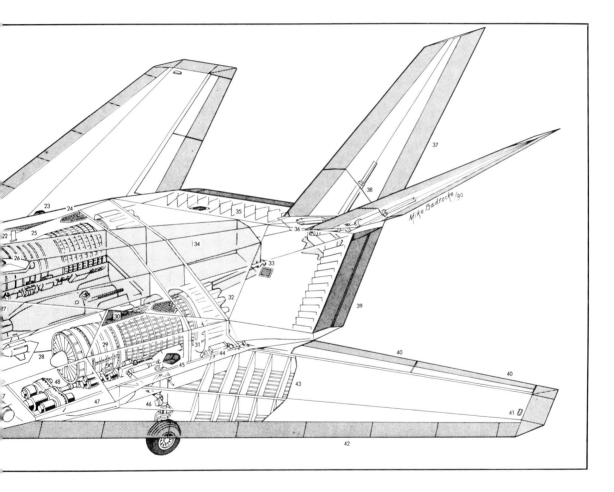

37	All-moving tailfins	**43**	Double-wedge wing section
38	Fin pivot bearing	**44**	Elevon hydraulic actuator
39	Upward canted platypus nozzle fairing	**45**	Radar augmentor
		46	Forward-retracting main undercarriage unit
40	Inboard and outboard elevons	**47**	Mainwheel bay
41	Retractable navigation lights, port and starboard	**48**	Airframe mounted accessory equipment gearbox
42	RAM coated surfaces		

cently, the USAF has amended that response to "a full range of tactical munitions," a less sweeping statement.

Specially developed or modified weapons could take many forms. However, it would not be surprising if some "launch and leave" weapons were avail-

The F–117A ejection seat is a McDonnell Douglas ACES II, with some parts repainted to avoid any visible glint. McDonnell Douglas/-Robert Arance

able as an alternative to the LGB, particularly for use against targets with very heavy point defenses. One possibility would be an IR-guided bomb, with a similar seeker to the AGM–65D Maverick. It would have to be dropped from an extendable rack, so that its seeker could be steered on to the aimpoint before release. Another option would be an inertially aided weapon: a glide bomb with a simple inertial guidance system which corrects the weapon's flight path to conform to the trajectory predicted by the launch aircraft's bombing computer.

It is not known whether the F–117A has been tested with air-to-air weapons. The lack of a radar makes it incompatible with the AIM–7 Sparrow, but it could be fitted with the AIM–9 Sidewinder if the mission called for the destruction of an airborne target. Like an IR-guided air-to-surface missile, it would have to be launched from an extendable mount to allow it to acquire its target before launch.

It was one thing to design a weapon such as the F–117A; it was quite another to make it work in service, and to bring it to a point where it was reliable enough to be entrusted with extremely sensitive missions. The process was to take a great deal of work, between 1983 and 1986.

Chapter 3

Tough training and hard lessons

Train the way you fight, and fight the way you train.

Military pilot's maxim

The F–117A was conceived black, it was built black and, as far as possible, it would fly and fight black. It was designed to perform covert missions which would certainly not be revealed before they took place and might not be revealed afterward. In that sense it was the same as the D–21 or the A–12.

The difference between the F–117A and its black predecessors was that the most sensitive features of the earlier aircraft were inside. The F–117A, by contrast, was quite conventional on the inside; its secrets were written in every line of its faceted outside shape.

Moreover, most sources of information on Stealth suggested that smoothly curved shapes, like the SR–71, were the key to ultra-low RCS. That the truth might be the diametrical opposite of this popular impression was, in the eyes of the Pentagon, a very valuable secret, and one which could be blown by one clear photograph of the F–117A.

Tonopah

Because of this, security considerations dominated the way the F–117 was to be used and deployed by the US Air Force. The first step was to find a base for the aircraft. Groom Lake was ruled out. It was ideal for flight-testing but had no facilities for an operational unit. There were also security concerns; most black aircraft projects used Groom Lake, and, inevitably, people on one project saw more details of other projects than they were supposed to see. As long as the Groom Lake crews were black-world specialists, this could be tolerated, but an operational unit would bring in many more people.

The USAF decided to build a new base for the F–117A on the Tonopah Test Range (TTR). The TTR abuts the northwestern corner of the Nellis complex and, before 1983, had mainly been used for drop-tests of nuclear weapons. During the peak of weapons testing, in the 1950s, Sandia Laboratories had built an airstrip at TTR to support its test activities. The new facility was planned around that strip.

TTR's proximity to the Nellis complex was important. Nellis is the largest area of government-owned, non-public land outside the Soviet Union or China; it is roughly the size of Switzerland. The aircraft would have plenty of room to operate unobserved, to fly against simulated radars and to drop weapons.

The site was not quite perfect from the security viewpoint, because the strip was overlooked by public land. On the other hand, it was not a place likely to draw the casual visitor. The nearest town was Tonopah itself, thirty-two miles northwest of the airstrip site. One of many silver-boom towns in the area, Tonopah supported 5,000 people but had been sagging since US Borax, the largest employer, closed its operations there. Other towns in the area were in tougher shape yet, hanging on to the remnants of gold-mining in the desert hills. There was no larger community

The new base at TTR is a large facility with fifty-four individual hangars spread over more than a mile of flight-line. The larger hangars beyond the control tower house maintenance facilities and, possibly, accommodate other programs. At the far end of the base is a parking area for transport aircraft. James C. Goodall

closer than Hawthorne, 100 miles farther up Nevada's State Highway 95, and the nearest major city, Las Vegas, was some 200 miles away.

Tonopah's remoteness and the small local population would make it very difficult for anybody to observe operations at the site without being observed themselves. Nevertheless, the USAF assumed that the outline of the F-117A would, sooner or later, be compromised—perhaps by a lucky shot with a camera, possibly by a determined enthusiast, possibly by an infra-red sensor on an unexpected satellite. To determine how much damage such a revelation would cause, the USAF took some plan-view impressions of the F-117 and showed them to some of its own intelligence analysts. Their first reaction was that they were

The off-base housing area is more than seven miles from the operating base and is linked to it by a bus shuttle. James C. Goodall

looking at a Mach 6 replacement for the SR-71. They were then told what the aircraft was and were asked to estimate its radar cross-section. Their estimates were too high, by a significant factor. The service's conclusion was that the project would not be seriously compromised by a quick glimpse of the aircraft.

In fact, the security surrounding the program was so effective that the location of the new base was not publicly reported until 1985, by which time a brand-new control tower, twenty individual hangars and other buildings had arisen beside a resurfaced 12,000-foot runway in the Nevada desert, and the

base had been operating for nearly two years.

Pilots

The USAF started to search for potential F-117 pilots in 1980, sifting through its records for candidates. The pilots selected for the first series of interviews shared some attributes. First, they were experienced in air-to-ground missions, having flown F-111s, F-4s or A-10s. Most were at about the same rank, middle to senior captains. All of them had at least 1,000 hours of flight time, mostly in fighter aircraft.

Later, Ben Rich of Lockheed stressed that the flying hours were required "not

Most 37th TFW personnel commute between Nellis AFB and TTR on Boeing 727s operated by Key Airlines. Key, with specially cleared pilots, also serves Burbank, Palmdale and Groom Lake. James C. Goodall

for experience, but for maturity." A former F-117 pilot describes the group as "calm people and decent pilots . . . They were all picked for flying ability and decision-making. They had to be able to weather through unknown emergencies."

At their interviews, the pilots were told the bare minimum about their mission. They were told that they would be flying A-7s (which was partly true) and that the posting would take them away from their families during the week. The candidates were given five minutes to decide whether to volunteer. If nothing else, this tested their ability to make critical decisions under stress. If they agreed, they were sent back to their units and told to wait for a call to action.

The senior commanders for the F-117 unit were, in USAF slang, "fast burners": officers on the way to becoming generals. According to one pilot, "they had a limited flying background but they had had a lot of staff jobs. They were good for a brand-new unit, where they had to put everything together, not just the flying operations. They were not especially good for the flyers."

Flight training

In most cases, the call came in mid-1982, as production aircraft began to roll off the line at Burbank. The F-117 was still less than halfway through its flight-test program, and the first pilots went through their initial ground school at the production site. "They taught you wiring diagrams, all that crap that we didn't care about," one pilot recalled. One of the first tasks faced by the initial group of operational pilots was to

From the formation of the 4450th TG in 1980 until November 1988, when the F-117A was declassified, the USAF maintained that it was a Nellis-based test unit equipped with

A-7Ds. The oversized unit number on this aircraft helped support that story. Kevin Patrick

develop a ground and flight training program for those who would follow them.

The USAF did not plan to buy the F-117 in large numbers, and so the cost of designing and building a two-seat training version was not considered justifiable. The pilot's first flight in the aircraft was also his first solo. (The same decision was made in the case of the U-2, the A-12 and the SR-71; in each case it was reversed, and trainers were produced by modifying in-service aircraft. This has not been done with the F-117.)

The first pilots practiced on a cockpit procedures trainer (CPT), a working model of the cockpit. Unlike a simulator or weapon system trainer (WST), the CPT does not move and it does not have a visual system to reproduce the view from the cockpit, so it is mainly used to familiarize the pilot with the operation of the aircraft's systems. The pilot cannot learn to fly the aircraft on the CPT.

Before making their first flights in the F-117, the first group of pilots took one ride in a two-seat F-15B. The reason was that the F-117's landing and take-off characteristics were fairly similar to those of the F-15, or were at least closer to those of the F-15 than to the A-10 or F-111.

As the number of USAF pilots entering the F-117 program began to increase, however, a more formal training program took effect. It also formed part of the security screen over the aircraft. A few LTV A-7D Corsair II attack aircraft were assigned to the F-117 program. When a pilot was making his first few F-117 flights, an experienced pilot would take off just before him in an A-7D, circle around the airfield and catch up with him as he took off. The instructor in the A-7D would follow the new pilot around the circuit, monitoring his speed and altitude and, as far as possible, evaluating his flying technique. The A-7Ds also provided the pilots with a chance to keep logging hours when few F-117s were available, and provided an element of cover for TTR. Asked what was based at TTR, the USAF could reply "A-7s."

4450th Tactical Group

The newly formed 4450th Tactical Group moved to Tonopah in 1983, with a force which probably amounted to a partial squadron of F-117s and a few A-7Ds. (The latter were assigned to the 4451st Tactical Squadron; the F-117 squadron designation is not known.) By that time, the first batch of twenty F-117s was close to complete. Four or five aircraft were still involved in flight tests at Groom Lake, and one aircraft (80-785) had been written off, so up to a dozen aircraft may have been available by the time the F-117 and the 4450th Tactical Group were declared, in October 1983, to have reached initial operational capability.

Meanwhile, a major change had taken place in the program. As *Senior Trend* had progressed, more key members of Congress—including the House and Senate armed services and appropriations committees—had been accessed into the program, permitting both the USAF and Lockheed to brief them. The response was more enthusiastic than the USAF had bargained for. Not only did the hard-line hawks like the F-117, but it also appealed to the "military reform" movement in Congress, because of its subtle use of high technol-

Since mid–1989, Northrop T–38s have been used by the F–117 unit as chase aircraft for training flights, for refresher training in daytime tactics—most F–117A pilots will go back to F–16s or F–15s after their tours are over—and to build up hours. Kevin Patrick

ogy, its utility in situations other than all-out conventional or nuclear war, and its unparalleled bombing accuracy. Instead of trimming the program, Congress directed the US Air Force to acquire an entire wing of F-117s, nominally consisting of four squadrons and seventy-two aircraft. The production line at Burbank kept moving, and more individual hangars were built at TTR. Two operational squadrons (identified by letters rather than numbers) were formed at TTR; one was known as the Nightstalkers, and the other as the Grim Reapers.

The phrase "initial operational capability," or IOC, is not very precise. It indicates that the system concerned and its operating unit could take some part in a war if one was to break out. Usually, however, the system is not ready to perform significant parts of the total spectrum of missions for which it was designed. This was the case with the F-117A. Testing at Groom Lake was continuing at IOC; as the test aircraft cleared a portion of the operational envelope, the operational pilots would incorporate it into their training syllabus. There were few aircraft available, so pilots flew the A-7Ds to remain proficient. For the first year of operations, too, the 4450th TG was confined to the Nellis range; technical problems were not uncommon, and the USAF wanted to avoid putting the aircraft down on a non-secure base if it could possibly be helped.

Operations training

The trends after IOC were all positive, though. More aircraft had been delivered; technical snags had been resolved, and the maintenance people had become more familiar with the aircraft. The F–117s were available on a regular schedule, more pilots were coming into the operation, and serious operational training and practice could begin. In 1984 and 1985, the 4450th TG was to establish a hard routine of training and practice that was to continue into the end of 1988.

The pilots' task was not easy. The F–117 was designed for nocturnal special operations, which are in many ways the most demanding of all military aviation missions. Special operations are often "one aircraft, one time" missions; the pilot operates autonomously, without back-up, knowing that if the operation fails, or the bomb falls in the wrong place, there is no other aircraft to com-

plete the mission. Moreover, the element of surprise is lost, the defenses are alert and the mission cannot be attempted again. The only way to establish confidence that such operations will work is by intense, realistic training.

While many fighters can and do operate at night, the F–117 is unique in that it would never be sent against a real target in daylight. Virtually all operational training, therefore, would be carried out at night; this was a particular challenge for fighter pilots, used to "eyeballs-out" flying.

Bombers and special-operations transports practice difficult autonomous missions at night, with the important distinction that they have several crew members on board to share tasks,

Rank has its privileges. Kevin Patrick

to monitor and to cross-check. The F–117 pilot is on his own, maintaining radio silence. The view from the cockpit is limited, and there is little to see in any case.

Security

Security considerations compounded the challenge. By 1984, the shape of the F–117 still had not been compromised in any way, and the USAF wanted to keep the aircraft from view. Daytime F–117 flights, usually in the first or last hours of daylight, were kept to the bare minimum required to train new pilots. For most of the day, an observer overlooking Tonopah would see only a brand-new air base which seemed mysteriously abandoned by all human life.

Security also dictated that only those people working on the program be housed at the site; there was no provision for families at TTR. Officers, including all the pilots, were housed with their families at Nellis AFB, 190 miles away at the opposite corner of the range, and commuted by air to work on Monday morning, returning on Friday.

Transport was provided by 727s belonging to Key Airlines, technically a civilian charter company that works largely for the Department of Defense. The 4450th TG also flew a Mitsubishi MU–2 turboprop to carry individuals or small groups between TTR and Nellis or the Las Vegas airport.

Another basic security rule was that hangar doors would never be

Inflight refueling from a KC–135 or a KC–10A is practiced frequently. Most refuelings are carried out at night, without lights and in radio silence, a demanding task for both the F–117A pilot and the "boomer" (boom operator) in the KC–10A. USAF photo by Eric Schulzinger of Lockheed

opened between half an hour before sunrise and half an hour after sunset. In summer, therefore, operational flying would not start until 9 pm. Because of the Monday-morning to Friday-morning schedule, a normal week at TTR had only four flying nights. As the pace of operations increased, it became normal for each available aircraft to fly two sorties each night. By the time the last aircraft to launch on its first sortie had landed from its second "go," it was often 3 am or later.

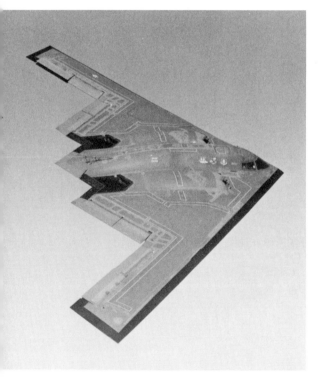

The F-117A proved that a Stealth aircraft could be built, could fly and could perform a combat mission, something that many people did not believe was possible. The F-117A made it possible for the USAF to plan and develop subsequent Stealth aircraft such as the Northrop B-2 bomber. USAF

Training sorties

Typically, the F-117 pilots would get up between 10 am and noon, taking recreation and relaxation at the start of the day. "We'd go out and play tennis for a couple of hours, unless it was snowing, then go eat lunch," one recalls. The first pilot on duty was the designated mission planner for that day, who would take the seven-mile bus ride from the housing area to the operations building at around 4 pm.

Planning

The TTR operations building is a windowless vault that houses briefing rooms, records and a formidable mission-planning computer system. A pilot recalls the mission-planning task: "I'd take a look at the weather and pick some routes for that night, depending on the moonlight and the weather conditions." Moonlight would mean avoiding populated areas, for security reasons.

The routes for a night's flying extended over much of the western United States, up to 300 miles from TTR. Most missions lasted about an hour and a half. Each route was a list of turn-points and targets, selected to hone the pilots' skills in navigation and finding pinpoint targets. The F-117s avoided major cities and dense concentrations of air traffic. Often (on about a quarter to a third of all sorties) the route would include an inflight-refueling rendezvous with a KC-135 or KC-10 tanker from March AFB or Castle AFB in California.

Several aircraft would follow the same route each night. Launching two to ten minutes apart, however, they might as well be alone. If the unit was launching more aircraft than one route could accommodate, a second route would be used, and it usually crossed the first. Launch times would be adjusted to "deconflict" the two. The F-117s were operating in public airspace, so Stealth was not an issue. Like other military aircraft, they carried transponders which would automatically identify them to military and civilian surveillance radar. F-117s also carried cobbled-on anticollision lights and passive radar reflectors on their fuselage sides. Here, too, they used the A-7s as a cover, all flights being identified as A-7s.

Briefing

Most of the pilots would reach the operations building between 1700 and 1800 hrs. Everybody who was flying that night was briefed at the same time (1830 hrs. in the summer); first weather, then the route and the launch times. The only unusual feature would be that the weatherman would give them both the weather on the target route and the current weather over a typical target such as Tehran or Damascus. Photographs of the target areas, acquired before the mission by satellites or other assets, would be shown. "On a real simple night, you could finish in twenty minutes, but it normally took thirty to forty minutes," a pilot recalls. "Then the guys go back to look at their targets and turn-points so they can identify them, do their own mission planning and the target study." The latter meant examining and memorizing details of the target, and any characteristic features around it which would help the pilot find it. "Then they would start going out to the airplanes."

Data transfer unit

Like many modern combat aircraft, the F-117 has a simple but immensely convenient device in the cockpit: a data

The Have Blue *patch shows cartoon character Wile E. Coyote holding a blue lightning flash, signifying control of the electromagnetic spectrum. (The Road Runner, the Coyote's uncatchable nemesis, had been the symbol of the Mach 3 Blackbird development program.)*

transfer unit (DTU). The DTU is a receptacle for an electronic memory cartridge, about the size of a cigarette pack, which stores turn-points and other vital information for the mission. The DTU cartridge can be programmed by the main mission-planning computer or by the pilot's own workstation. Either method is much easier than entering all the same information on the tiny keys in the confines of the cockpit.

Aligning INS

Each aircraft at TTR has its own hangar. Most USAF aircraft in the continental United States are parked out of doors, but the F-117s had their own hangars to protect them from observation by satellites in the daytime. By the time each pilot reached his airplane, it would have been checked out and "powered up" from an electrical hook-up. The pacing item was the need to start the alignment of the inertial navigation system (INS). Like any complex

Two of the F–117A flight test patches. Flight-test crews on the F–117A program conferred the nickname "Scorpion" on the F–117A. FTE stands for "flight test and evaluation"; the legend on the other patch refers to Baja (lower, or southern) Groom Lake, where the F–117 FTE group was located.

mechanical device, the INS contains small biases which tend to average out over time, and it also needs some time to reach an equal operating temperature. Aligning the INS (letting it run while the aircraft is in a precisely known position) ensures that the system will operate as accurately as possible.

Once the INS was aligned, the F-117 was usually ready to go within minutes. "You would do your pre-flight inspection, climb in, start out on time and out you go."

Flying the sortie

The F-117 is not a difficult aircraft to fly in classic stick-and-rudder terms, a characteristic which its pilots attribute to the effectiveness of its fly-by-wire flight control system. "Smooth. It is the smoothest-flying airplane I have ever been in, smoother than the F-15," commented one pilot. If it has one weakness, it is that it is not overpowered. Out of TTR, 6,000 feet above sea level, on a hot day with a fully loaded aircraft, an engine failure could be more than embarrassing. But most training flights start 4,000 pounds below maximum take-off weight, with an empty weapon bay, at cooler nighttime temperatures. The F-117 does not have the rocket-like climb of an F-16 or F-15, but gets to altitude at a respectable speed.

Most of the mission was flown at an efficient cruising altitude, between 25,000 and 30,000 feet, dropping down to make the final run on the target. The F-117 is not designed or equipped for low-level terrain-following flight, and its altitude at weapon release depends on a number of factors. These include the weather (because the effective range of the infra-red sensors is affected by humidity) and the nature of the target.

If the target is hard to pick out from the background, the pilot may come in higher, because that gives him more time to look for it.

Finding the target

The biggest single influence on the attack profile, however, is the air defense threat. One of TTR's biggest computers contains the location of every known air defense radar in the world. It runs software that computes the range at which the radar can detect the F-117 at different angles and heights. In some cases, the best tactic is to skirt the radar's envelope of coverage; in others, it is actually better to head straight toward the radar and present it with the F-117's tiny frontal RCS. If the radar itself is the target, a dive attack could be the best approach. Alternatively, the F-117 might drop to low altitude in the final stages of the attack, using terrain to screen itself from the radar.

Once airborne, the pilot's task was to be in exactly the right place at exactly the right time, navigating with the INS and using the electro-optical sensors to confirm turn-points and identify targets. Thermal images have their own characteristics. Says a pilot: "The hardest stuff was cold things. Buildings where people lived and there was heat, you could find. Bridges were fairly easy. The hardest things were manmade structures, like a fire warden's shack on a mountain in the trees. There wasn't much heat coming out of that thing, and it might be covered with snow, and it might not be exactly on top of the mountain although the map shows a little symbol sitting on top of a hill. You might get within a mile of it; now you have to search that area, trying to find the cold object in the middle of the woods." Such targets might seem unrealistically small, but the 4450th TG was developing the ability to go after targets such as bunkers, which might be buried under inconspicuous landmarks. After a time, the pilot recalls, "We picked hard things because the normal targets were easy."

Patches worn by USAF and Lockheed personnel in support of the F-117A program.

Most missions included turn-points and two targets—one for each weapon on the F-117—but on some nights the planners scheduled a "turkey shoot" with up to fourteen targets to be found and identified. The pilot who came back with the best FLIR videotape was the night's winner. "Some of them were real minuscule, piss-ant targets such as an intersection of a couple of dirt roads in the middle of nowhere. One of the hardest was a dock on the Marina at Lake Tahoe. That was a bitch and I don't know if anyone did find that. The water is so cold that it didn't show up at all."

Some targets were on weapons ranges. The F-117s used the Nellis complex and the USAF ranges north of Edwards AFB, around Mountain Home AFB in Idaho, and in Utah, the Navy's ranges at Fallon, near Reno, and China Lake in California. On the ranges, the pilots could use the laser to illuminate a target; use of the laser off-range was forbidden.

Inflight refueling

Two 4450th TG patches. The "Goat Sucker" emblem is an early 4450th TG patch, possibly helping to support the cover mission of the A-7s. At the time, the F-117A was nicknamed the "Nighthawk" by the operational crews; and, as any ornithologist will tell you, the North American nighthawk is also called the goatsucker.

For each pilot, one mission per week would include an inflight refueling. Normally, USAF fighter pilots refuel three times in each six months, but the 4450th TG did more, partly for their own sake but also to train a group of "boomers," the operators of the refueling boom on the tanker aircraft, in the special techniques required to refuel the F-117. "It was all done lights-out, and no talking," a pilot says. The F-117 carried no lights except one small, aft-facing lamp on top of the cockpit which illuminated the refueling receptacle in the top of the fuselage, and the tanker would turn off everything except its top beacon and a small light underneath. The poor upward view from the F-117A's cockpit compounded the problem; when the boom was in place, the pilot could not see it at all. "When there was a moon, you could see everything; on moonless nights it was tough."

Without radio, timing was everything: a successful refueling depended on the tanker and the F-117 being in the right place at the right time. If necessary, the F-117 pilot could use his FLIR to search for the tanker (it has a range of tens of miles in the clear air at 30,000 feet) and close in until the boomer could see the black shape below him and aim the boom at the small light on the fighter. Even then, on a moonless night, either the tanker or the F-117 could be swallowed by a cloud at any moment, without the least warning. "There were times that guys would miss the tanker during their first few refuelings, but it could happen any time," a pilot says.

Emergency plans

Missions were set up so that a missed refueling would leave the aircraft with enough fuel to make TTR. In a more serious emergency, the pilot might have to land at another USAF base. As soon as the F-117s started to fly outside the Nellis range, base commanders in the western United States were told that, some night, a classified aircraft might land at their facilities. The F-117 pilots carried a letter, signed by a senior USAF officer, which one pilot has paraphrased as "Do what this guy says, and call me in the morning." The base commander was to make a hangar available for the F-117A, and secure it under armed guard. Anyone on the base who saw it or knew of its arrival had to sign a statement that they would say nothing about the night's events. As far as is known, this procedure has never been used.

Mission over, the pilots would return to TTR, practice a couple of instrument approaches, if there was fuel remaining and not too many other aircraft doing the same thing in the dark desert sky, and land. The first job after climbing out

Before 1989, the 4450th TG included two operational squadrons, the Nightstalkers

and the Grim Reapers. Squadron numbers were never assigned.

of the airplane was to debrief with the maintenance crew on any problems with the aircraft. "Then get a ride to the ops building, take off your boots and helmet and put it away. Then you would look at your tape—your mission—to see if you did indeed identify everything." Videotape and the FLIR have replaced the gun and bomb cameras of older days, creating an instant and very honest record of the pilot's success in locating his targets.

Daily routine

Typically, in summer, a dozen aircraft would be launched on the night's first sortie, the "early-go." The first would be on the ground by 2230 hrs. and the last by 0030 hrs. As the aircraft landed, the maintenance crews would refuel them and prepare them for the "late-go," the night's second sortie, which would start launching at midnight. Usually, pilots flew only one sortie per night, although "the guy who flew the first flight of the first go may have another flight on the second." The last of the second wave would be off by 0130 hrs. 'We tried to have everybody on the ground between 0230 and 0300 hrs. in the winter," a pilot says. "We would have to sometimes fly a little later than that in the summer."

The pilots who had landed would be busy with the same routine chores that occupy much of any military pilot's time: arranging flying and training schedules or writing reports. "You did your normal daily activities at night, which you would have done after a normal afternoon of flying." The last pilot of the second wave would finish his debrief by 0400 hrs. Then "everybody would head for home, probably head for the bar for a drink or

two, or head to bed." Some pilots would go for breakfast instead.

The routine was exhausting, not so much because of the hours of work but because of the shift in the pilots' body clocks. "When you get out and climb into the airplane, your adrenaline is so high that you don't get tired when you are flying, but then you land and it is 3 am and you get real tired . . . The bad part was that you come home on Friday, and have normal days over the weekend," a pilot says. "You had to change your body clock eight to nine hours every week. You get used to it, but you get a little more tired as the week goes on. Monday wasn't too bad, but by Thursday morning you were a wreck." According to Ben Rich, the experience can be compared with "flying to Korea for work every Monday, operating on Korean time during the week, and then returning home for the weekend, only to repeat the process starting the next Monday."

The USAF learned a lot about jet-lag. "We found that the daylight/darkness cycles accentuated the body-clock shift," says Ben Rich. "If a pilot was up all night and saw the sun come up, his mind would interpret daylight as time for the body to be active, and it was nearly impossible after that to enter a deep, restful sleep. You would have thought you were at a vampire convention as daybreak approached, watching all the night workers scurrying for their blacked-out rooms before they were caught by the sun."

Pilot fatigue

The chronically jet-lagged pilots found family life was disrupted. A posting with the 4450th TG "was almost a guaranteed divorce," one says. But fatigue could be lethal, particularly combined with what Ben Rich has called "the typical, macho fighter-pilot attitude that 'it's not manly to say you're too tired to fly.'" The pilots' perspective was different. "The original [squadron] was fifteen guys, all hand-picked and raring to go. It was like a flying club. We didn't have any rules or regulations until we started crashing airplanes."

The USAF brought extra flight surgeons into the program to investigate fatigue among the pilots, concerned that the problem was being underreported. Their studies intensified in the summer of 1986, as the increasing pace of operations coincided with shorter summer flying hours. In a memo dated July 10, Lt. Col. John F. Miller warned that "if we liken our usual late-go to a time-bomb

The 37th TFW patch is adapted from the original 4450th TG patch, with a different background. The 415th TFS retains the name Nightstalkers; the second operational squadron, now the 416th TFS, has become the Ghost Riders, with a symbolic F–117 in the background. The 417th TFTS, the training unit, are the Bandits, and their emblem is adapted from the original 417th Night Fighter Squadron's crest.

waiting to go off, then our extended summer hours are accelerating the countdown to zero. I believe we are on collision course with a mishap." Miller recommended that the USAF "force extra time off every two or three weeks," possibly an indication that it was the pilots, not the commanders, who were pushing the pace.

Miller dated his memo on a Thursday, just before the last flying night of the week. That night, Major Ross E. Mulhare was suiting-up for a late-go mission and told a colleague that he was tired and "just couldn't shake it." Mulhare's flight was one of the last to leave, at 1:13 am.

The first crash

That night's route went south and west over the Sierras, south over California's San Joaquin Valley and southeast toward the weapon ranges at Edwards. As the pilots made the easterly turn, the lights of Bakersfield disappeared and were replaced by the darkness of the mountains around Tehachapi.

Around 1:45 am, Mulhare's F-117 dived into a hillside in the Sequoia National Forest, seventeen miles northeast of Bakersfield. Mulhare made no attempt to eject and was killed. Campers in the park heard the engines until the moment of impact. The F-117 disintegrated on impact into pieces which were mostly the size of half-dollars; the flight data recorder was also destroyed.

Investigators later surmised that Mulhare had become disorientated during the turn to the southeast. Pilots at night have been known to confuse lights on the ground with the stars, even flying inverted for minutes at a time without being aware of it. At that point, it is easy to enter a dive and extremely difficult to focus on the instruments and return to a proper attitude. On the F-117, the problem is compounded by the fact that the unusual air-data system does not function properly above Mach 1. If, as seems likely, Mulhare's aircraft went supersonic in its dive, attitude and airspeed data would have been degraded, making a recovery almost impossible.

Contingency plans for an accident outside USAF property had been in place since operations started. An aircraft accident and subsequent fire were reported shortly after Mulhare's aircraft vanished from radar. The two events were quickly related by military controllers, and the incident was reported to Nellis AFB. A USAF security team was flown by helicopter from Nellis to the crash site, and they immediately declared it a national security area. Firefighters had to sign statements promising to say nothing of what they had seen.

The crash site remained closed for several weeks, while the USAF combed the area inch by inch, searching for shards of the secret RAM. Once the site was pronounced clean, a few fragments from a wrecked F-101 Voodoo fighter were buried in the area, to confuse any treasure-hunters.

There was no sign that the F-117 operation was curtailed or restricted in any way after the Mulhare accident, although there is no doubt that fatigue was taken a great deal more seriously. Later, Ben Rich was to comment that, in the F-117 world, "It is considered a sign of strength to admit that you're not ready to fly." In fact, the 4450th TG had completed its most arduous phase of training and was ready to go to war.

Chapter 4

Out of the black

"We're like the rabbi who gets a hole in one on Saturday."

Ben Rich, explaining his inability to discuss the F–117

Major Mulhare's crash near Bakersfield did nothing to lift the shroud of secrecy around the F-117, but it broke the silence that had surrounded it. The abrupt seizure of National Park land by a squad of heavily armed USAF men could not be suppressed or downplayed. National news organizations were on to the story before noon the next day, combing through files for references to the Stealth fighter or "F-19." The USAF gave Mulhare's name, unit and service record, but refused to identify the type of aircraft involved. Inside sources shut up like clams. Most newspapers published photographs of an entirely fictitious model of the "F-19," produced by the Testor Corporation.

Most readers had not known—and would barely have believed—that the USAF had developed and deployed a radical new warplane in almost total secrecy. What *nobody* knew was that the Stealth fighter had nearly gone to war. By mid-1986, F-117s had been armed and ready to launch on two covert combat missions. The targets are classified, but could have been terrorist headquar-

ters in the Middle East or Libya. (Conventional USAF and Navy units had hit Libyan targets in April 1986.) Both missions were canceled within hours of take-off.

Finding work

Like a Strategic Air Command bomber wing, the 4450th TG was on a war footing. Several F-117s were kept on alert at all times; their radar-absorbent skins were touched up and all systems were freshly overhauled, regularly tested and operational. These aircraft were not used for nightly training exercises, but were available for operational missions as soon as the pilots could be briefed and the INS aligned.

A task challenging USAF planners was finding a mission for the large force of F-117s authorized by Congress. The twenty aircraft ordered at the start of the program were enough to ensure that a handful of aircraft would be fully mission-ready at any time, for individual, covert strikes. Considering that not all of the aircraft would be available at any given time, and that the total included an allowance for noncombat losses, it is clear that no one envisaged needing any more than ten F-117s, at the most, on any one mission.

The F-117's capabilities are unique. No other aircraft can penetrate defenses undetected, deliver weapons with laser-guided accuracy, and return with videotape that shows the target has been hit. Like any weapon, however, the F-117 has its drawbacks. It has—as far as is known—no radar, so it can operate only in clear weather. It relies solely on its Stealth qualities for protection, and it is not invisible, so it operates only at night. Even then, it would be risky to use the F-117 under certain conditions of weather or lighting. The aircraft would not be sent out on a moonlit night above an undercast, or sent against city targets below the cloudbase. The F-117 therefore lends itself to the attack, because the attacker chooses the time of battle.

Without gaining access to highly classified war plans, it is possible to identify a number of generic scenarios in which the F-117 could be a potent player.

Surgical strike

One of these could be the classic "surgical strike," although that is a misnomer; bombs are never surgical, and all one can hope to do is be as accurate as possible. Typical objectives could be missile sites that are directly threatening an ally, a US installation or sea traffic. Other targets could be more strategic in nature, such as a plant producing nuclear or chemical weapons for use against an ally.

Hostage rescue

Another example is a Tehran-type situation, in which hostages are being held with the consent of the local gov-ernment. Their location is known. A careful disinformation program involving international mediators and diplomatic feelers has been carried out, and the local government and the hostage-takers are increasingly confident that their conditions for the return of the hostages will be met.

US special-operations forces are well equipped with transports and helicopters (the choice depends on distance and the availability of a runway) but none of them is designed or equipped for air combat. The operation can be carried out only if the local air defenses can be disabled quickly, thoroughly and without warning.

The attack involves a half-dozen pairs of F-117s (each pair includes a primary and a back-up). Satellite and human intelligence has been used to prepare target imagery, and the crews brief with information that is no more than hours old. Following separate tracks to their targets, to avoid alerting any ground observer by the sound of a large formation overhead, the F-117s reach their different objectives within seconds of each other. Most of the targets are surveillance radars, hit with conventional blast warheads, and surface-to-air missile sites, disabled with cluster and fragmentation weapons. Laser-guided penetrators slam into the runways at the air force's fighter bases, forcing the interceptors to sit on the ground until huge slabs of broken concrete can be cut up and removed.

Air force commanders are still yelling down dead telephones, trying to assess the extent of the damage, as the MC-130 Combat Talon transports and AC-130 Spectre gunships appear over the horizon and race for the rescue site.

As the troops land, another laser-guided bomb hits an electric substation and all the lights go out.

Coup d'etat

Another type of operation is aimed at a leader whose activities in support of terrorists or drug-runners have finally outworn the patience of the United States. A credible faction has offered to remove him, but without some assistance their chances are no better than even.

In this case, the targets are the command, control, communications and intelligence (C3I) structure—the telephone exchange, nodes in the electrical system, the headquarters of the armed forces and the political police and the radio and TV broadcasting centers. There are two rules: don't hit anything that isn't a target, and don't get shot down. If these two rules are followed, there is no conclusive evidence that any aircraft of any nationality was involved at all, and the well-coordinated blasts will bolster the impression that the coup leaders have the upper hand.

This is an extremely difficult mission to plan and execute. Some of the targets are city buildings. Even with a careful selection of turn-points and a last-minute INS update, the pilots are going to have to search their screens carefully and learn and identify features that are unique to their targets and surroundings. Despite any pressure to the contrary, the pilots must realize that it is better to drop ordnance in the water than to release against a target that has not been positively identified.

Any air defenses must be defeated through Stealth alone, because direct suppression will betray the fact that strike aircraft were involved. This means a great deal of intelligence-gathering, modeling and simulation to select ingress tracks which present the fighters' best profile to the particular radars in use.

There are some common points in both these scenarios. In both cases, the political will to conduct such missions is assumed. Stealth technology is applied to gain and hold the element of surprise. And in both cases, the main targets are assumed to be fixed. Also, neither of them requires a large force of aircraft, and it is difficult to envisage a situation where a large force of F-117s would be needed. This would happen only in a more intense, more wide-ranging conflict, but at that point, the commander is less free to choose a time and place to use the F-117s, and the opponent may be protecting more of his assets through mobility.

War in Europe

The entire *Senior Trend* operation has been controlled at the White House level since its inception. The F-117 was not intended to operate with other Tactical Air Command assets in an all-out war. In Central Europe, for example, the F-117 might be useful but could not always be relied on. In particular, its effectiveness would be much reduced in cloud and rain, because its infra-red sensors would have trouble locating its targets. Central Europe is also so full of targets and hostiles that even the F-117 might be detected visually, at random, unless it was operating under ideal visual conditions, with a clear night and no moon. But the Supreme Allied Commander, Europe (SACEUR) has never been in a position to decide when the war is going to start. The assumption, since 1945, has been that such a decision will be taken on the other side of the fence. In fact, none of the USAF commanders in chief, including the commander of US Air Forces, Europe (USAFE), was fully briefed on the F-117's capabilities.

One outcome of the debate over the F-117's role was that Congressional plans for the aircraft were scaled back. It was reported in late 1986 that the total order had been reduced from more than 100 to about sixty; in fact, the final buy settled at fifty-nine aircraft. By mid-1986, about thirty-five to forty of the aircraft had been delivered, with a few aircraft remaining at Groom Lake and the rest at TTR, and deliveries were running at about seven aircraft per year. Major maintenance was subcontracted to Lockheed at Palmdale.

The emphasis on night operations and security continued after 1986, as the tempo of operations continued to rise along with the number of aircraft and pilots involved. In 1985-87, the initial cadre of F-117 pilots rotated out of the system at the end of their four-year postings, to be replaced by three-year pilots.

Operational changes

Only one part of the basic operational concept has changed since the start of development. Although the F-117 is designed to be easily airlifted to an overseas operation location in a C-5, the USAF decided to fly the aircraft to the base from which it would hit its target, with the aid of inflight refueling. The 4450th TG carried out regular endurance flights over Nellis, refueling several times and flying for twelve hours or more, to prove that the aircraft would be reliable enough to do it. The USAF describes the F-117's range as "unlimited." In fact, human endurance is probably the limiting factor.

Overseas

As far as is known, the F-117 has not been deployed outside the United States, and it is not known whether it had ever landed at any base other than TTR or Groom Lake before its public debut at Nellis 17 April 1990. Some 4450th TG pilots flew the unit's A-7Ds to potential overseas operating locations, including USAF bases in the United Kingdom, to gain experience with different weather and terrain. Special security precautions were taken in the United Kingdom, which has a large fraternity of dedicated aircraft-spotters. The LV tail codes (for Las Vegas, or Nellis) immediately marked the A-7Ds for special attention, because no known Nellis-based unit (indeed, no regular USAF unit) operated the A-7D. When the A-7Ds visited the United Kingdom, ground crews took special pains to throw a cover over the underwing "TDY store" (a pod which provides space for personal belongings). Spotters assumed that the A-7s were testing some kind of classified sensor and did not immediately link them to the Stealth project.

There appears, however, to be a formal and secret agreement between the US and British governments covering the use of the F-117 from USAF bases in England. The evidence for this is that at least one Royal Air Force pilot has been attached to the 4450th TG, something that would be most unlikely in the absence of any reciprocal concession by Britain.

Lifting the veil

Although the Stealth fighter and its base were open secrets after Mulhare's accident, the USAF still did not acknowledge their existence, and the sporadic daylight operations at TTR did not provide many opportunities for visiting observers to see the aircraft. By this time, too, some 800 people from the city of Tonopah were working at TTR. They saw the F-117 regularly, and so did many residents of Tonopah and the surrounding communities. But Tonopah had long been accustomed to secret government activities, and its residents had broken themselves of habits such as asking questions and talking to outsiders. The owner of the local paper, the *Tonopah Times-Bonanza*, said later: "We wait for the news releases. We never press [the Air Force] to tell us anything." The newspaper never tried to photograph the F-117. "We've all seen it," commented the owner. "I don't know what purpose it would serve."

Others, however, wondered what purpose was being served by continued secrecy. During 1988, the veil was gradually lifted on the B-2 Stealth bomber, for which the F-117 had broken the trail. An artist's impression of the B-2 was released in April, more details followed as the year went on, and plans for its public roll-out were well under way. The B-2 was generally considered to represent a later generation of Stealth technology than the F-117. So why should the older aircraft be considered more secret?

Defense Secretary Caspar Weinberger resisted pressure to unveil the F-117. "Why give the Soviets information on a program that we spent a great deal of money developing?" he was to comment later, after leaving office. Others, including former Republican defense secretary James Schlesinger, suggested that the Reagan Administration as a whole was over enthusiastic about black programs, both out of an emotional fascination with security and as a means to forestall public debate about high-budget projects.

As the operational force passed fifty aircraft, however, the restrictions on day flying and on the use of bases other than TTR came to be a serious drag on the operation. Because the F-117s could not operate or train with other friendly forces in Red Flag or other combined-force exercises, it was almost impossible for commanders to write them into their war plans; they had no direct experience of what the 4450th could or could not do. Also, as the number of aircraft increased, so did the number of pilots. The consequent increase in the training load was exacerbated by the change from a four-year to a three-year posting. Assuming that the F-117 force had 1.25 pilots for each aircraft, it would have had to train eleven pilots in 1986 and twenty-two in 1988.

Fatigue was still a problem. The 4450th TG suffered its second F-117 fatality on October 14, 1987. Maj. Michael C. Stewart departed from TTR at 7:53pm and crashed into gently sloping ground on the Nellis range about forty minutes later. Like Mulhare, Stewart made no attempt to eject and the aircraft was totally destroyed. The investigation focused, once again, on crew fatigue and disorientation. It was a clear night with no moon and there were no lights to distinguish the ground. The mission included some special requirements (deleted from the first, unclassified page of the accident report), and the pilots were advised at their briefing that "if [two to three words deleted] was causing undue pressure, to [two to three words deleted] and to concentrate on aircraft control." Once again, however, no substantial changes in operations were observed after the accident.

By September 1988, reports had been going the rounds for months that the F-117 might be revealed in the run-up to the presidential election if the Republican lead seemed vulnerable. By October 2, an announcement seemed imminent. According to the *Los Angeles Times*, Defense Secretary Frank Carlucci was ready to authorize a release, but was warned off by Democrats Sam Nunn and Les Aspin (chairmen, respectively, of the Senate and House Armed Services Committees). The spectre of the 1980 campaign had come back to haunt the Republicans; Nunn and Aspin warned Carlucci that they and the Dukakis/Bentsen campaign would charge the Republicans with compromising national security for political ends. By October 5, nobody would admit that any announcement had even been contemplated.

The announcement was delayed, instead, until November 10, just after the election and almost exactly ten years after the *Senior Trend* project started. It was a muted affair, distinguished by one last attempt at disinformation: the issue of a single grainy, over-contrasty, heavily edited photograph, taken with a telephoto lens from an angle that drastically foreshortened the aircraft.

Officially, the Pentagon said that it was revealing the aircraft so that it could be more fully integrated with other assets. The most visible effect of the revelation, however, was that the 4450th TG greatly intensified its daytime operations. By the spring of 1989, F-117s were operating almost continuously from TTR.

Day flying

Now, transitioning F-117A pilots fly the aircraft during all daytime hours, flying out of TTR and using the ranges around the airfield. They then switch to night flying with an operational squadron and are designated combat-ready after a tactical flight evaluation. Once combat-ready, they fly about two-thirds of their sorties at night. It is not known exactly how this is arranged, but it is a fair guess that pilots now spend one week in three working on normal local time, giving their body clocks a valuable respite. Inflight refueling is still practiced frequently.

Because the F-117As could now be operated from other locations, the A-7D was no longer needed as a substitute when pilots needed to train in other environments. Neither was the A-7D needed as a cover for night operations. The 4450th TG still required chase aircraft for training, but the Northrop T-38, the standard USAF advanced trainer, was simpler and less costly to operate than the A-7. The T-38 replaced the A-7D in the summer of 1989, and the 4451st TS was officially "inactivated" on August 4.

37th Tactical Fighter Wing

By that time, the *Senior Trend* operation had, for practical purposes, a full complement of aircraft. Four or five aircraft remained to be delivered, but they could be regarded as attrition replacements. A symbol of that fact was a change in unit designation, which took effect in October 1989. The 4450th TG was renamed the 37th Tactical Fighter Wing, adopting the wing designator formerly used by the Wild Weasel force at George AFB. The two operational squadrons, previously unnumbered, were designated the 415th and 416th Tactical Fighter Squadrons, and the training unit was designated the 417th Tactical Fighter Training Squadron.

All three squadron numbers had been originally assigned in February 1943 to some of the US Army Air Force's first night-fighter squadrons. They trained in the United States on the Douglas P-70 (a modification of the A-20 Havoc bomber), but first went into combat with British-built Bristol Beaufighters, mounting aggressive night intruder operations over Italy and France. The emblem of the 417th TFTS is almost prophetic: a white ghost riding a rocket. "The ghost is representative of the element of surprise," reads the description, approved in 1953. "The rocket is indicative of the internal stores utilized by fighter-bombers."

Program cost

The capital cost of building all fifty-nine aircraft was $6,560.3 million in "then-year" dollars (outlays in the years in which the money was spent). This program cost breaks down as follows: research and development for the F-117A cost $1,999.6 million. Procurement, including the total cost of building fifty-nine aircraft, initial spares, and specialized ground support and training equipment (the mission planning system alone is believed to have cost almost $1,000 million) accounted for $4,265.3 million, and the new base at Tonopah cost $295.4 million.

The total "flyaway cost"—the cost of building the fifty-nine fully equipped aircraft, less tooling—was $2,514.6 billion, or $42.6 million for each aircraft. This is roughly comparable to the flyaway cost of an F-15E ($50.4 million in 1991 dollars), an aircraft which has been built at a much higher and more economical rate.

Panama

The 37th TFW went into action at the end of 1989. In 1988, as the US Administration's list of available political options to deal with Gen. Manuel Noriega's regime in Panama began to dwindle, the Pentagon's list of military options began to grow. USAF planners with access to *Senior Trend* were involved in the process and identified a range of targets the F-117 could attack.

The Stealth capabilities of the F-117 were not particularly important in Panama. The Panamanian Defense Force (PDF) had no serious ability to defend Panamanian airspace, and F-111s or A-6s could have attacked at low level and achieved equal surprise. However, what was most important was the F-117's unique ability to place weapons reliably and accurately on target.

Early on the night of December 19, six F-117s took off from TTR and headed southeast. Reports that the aircraft staged through bases in Texas or Florida should be taken with a grain of salt. The F-117A was entirely capable of performing the mission non-stop with tanker support, and the convenience of eliminating a tanker mission could be more than offset by the inconvenience of added security precautions.

The force probably comprised three pairs, one of each pair being the primary attacker and the other being the backup. Some of the aircraft are believed to have been assigned to contingency targets which, in the event, did not have to be attacked. In that event, only one of the aircraft released weapons, dropping two laser-guided 2,000 pound bombs at about 0100 hrs. on open ground immediately adjacent to the PDF base at Rio Hato. The bombs have been described as "the world's largest stun grenades"; they were not intended to kill anyone or damage occupied buildings, but to confuse and distract the PDF troops. In the few minutes it took the PDF to determine the source of the explosions, troops of the 82nd Airborne Division parachuted into Rio Hato, attacked the base and overran it, taking most of the PDF force prisoner and seizing most of the weapons on the site.

The Panama mission was promptly attacked by some critics as a publicity stunt, a suggestion vehemently denied some weeks later by TAC commander General Robert D. Russ. "We picked the best aircraft for the job, and it did it perfectly," Russ told an Air Force Association group in Orlando. "If you're going into a fight, why pick the second-best aircraft? Then you get a bloody nose, and everyone says: 'You dummy, why didn't you use the best you had?'"

Apparently, one or more of the bombs struck significantly off their planned targets. Based on this, some critics have charged that the F-117 is at fault. The USAF claims that the bombs struck where they were aimed, but that the pilot's aim was at fault. At the time of this writing, the controversy continues.

The future

A significant change in the *Senior Trend* program was announced at the end of January 1990: the 37th TFW is to move from TTR to Holloman AFB, New Mexico, replacing a T-38 unit. Some new construction will be needed at Holloman, probably including individual hangars, a secure operations building and a new RAM-respraying facility. Work will start in 1991, so the move will not take place until 1992 at the earliest. In the long run, the initial cost of the move and new construction will be recovered by eliminating the 727 shuttle between Nellis and TTR.

As the move takes place, according to TAC's General Russ, "There's got to be some declassification. We're bringing the F-117 out of the closet." Holloman, like most domestic USAF bases, is not a highly secure facility.

TTR is not being closed, according to USAF budget documents, although the 37th TFW and associated activities are the only known occupants of the base. It is probable that the base will continue to be used for covert activities as other "black" programs transition from testing at Groom Lake to operational status.

Only two F-117As remained to be delivered as these words are written, and they will probably have left Burbank by the time this book appears. The defense budget is being cut. The Berlin Wall is down. The threat of nuclear war has receded, as has the threat of a Europe-wide conventional war. All the assumptions on which the United States bases its military policies are changing. Attempting to predict the shape and size of the US armed services in the year 2,000 is an exercise for the brave or the foolhardy.

How the F-117 will fit into these forces is uncertain. Tactical Air Command's response to shrinking budgets has been to accept the elimination or shrinkage of some of its minor missions, in order to save money for its primary tactical fighter wings. Counter-air F-15s, multi-role F-16s and the interdiction force of F-111s and F-15Es are preserved. But the F-4G Wild Weasels are to be eliminated, and the tactical reconnaissance mission may be assigned to the Air National Guard or the USAF Reserves. If budgets are squeezed tighter, TAC may have to decide whether keeping the F-117 is worth the loss of a conventional fighter wing.

New Stealth replacement

In fact, the F-117's replacement may already be in production. The US Navy's A-12 Advanced Tactical Aircraft, being built by General Dynamics and McDonnell Douglas, appears in some respects to be an updated F-117. Using a later generation of Stealth technology, the A-12 has similar engines to the F-117 (GE F412-GE-400s, an uprated version of the F404) but its weapon load and range are in the class of the A-6 or F-111. In addition to a comprehensive electro-optical suite (the best built-in system of any aircraft except the F-117) it has a high-resolution, low-probability-of-intercept radar, and it has a crew of two with extremely modern cockpit displays. The USAF plans to acquire A-12s to replace its F-111s, and, assuming that its Stealth qualities are on the same order as the Lockheed aircraft, it may replace the F-117 as well.

Under the review of aircraft programs in April 1990, however, the USAF's A-12 purchases were delayed until at least 1997. It is almost certain that the A-12 will not be procured in sufficient quantities to replace the F-117 until well after the year 2000. This strengthens the case for those who suggest improvements, such as a radar system, for the F-117.

Conclusion

But neither the A-12, nor the Northrop B-2, nor the Advanced Tactical Fighter, would exist at all were it not for *Have Blue* and *Senior Trend*. *Have Blue* proved that an ultra-low-observable vehicle could fly. *Senior Trend* proved that a Stealth aircraft could perform a combat mission. Both these facts were doubted by many knowledgeable people; it took concrete results to get Stealth technology into so many missions.

In 1975, the survival of any Western air force against barrages of advanced Soviet SAMs seemed to be in serious doubt. The SA-6 was hard enough to beat, but its replacement, the SA-11, was already under development. The Soviet Union was pumping enormous resources into radar-guided SAMs, from the highly mobile SA-8 to the hypersonic SA-10. The West has, in general, not matched these systems because the cost of deploying them to cover the entire battle area is not affordable.

But the radar-guided SAM was based on one unquestioned premise: that aircraft had a radar cross-section of at least five square meters and that they would always have so. The Skunk Works engineers and the 4450th TG demolished that premise.

By the early 1980s, Soviet planners realized that they would soon have to contend with an increasing number of targets their thousands of SAMs could not touch, including aircraft which threatened the Soviet homeland itself and would negate the Soviet Union's elite air-defense forces.

No doubt there was, and is, a plan to revamp the battlefield and strategic air-defense systems to deal more effectively with Stealth targets. The USAF has one, called the Air Defense Initiative (ADI). It would be enormously expensive, and there is no sign that either ADI or its Soviet equivalent will be put into place. Under Mikhail Gorbachev, the Soviet Union is slowing its military production and changing its military posture to one that does not seem as threatening to the West.

The revolution in the Communist bloc had many causes. Unquestionably, though, one of the most important was the failure of the Comecon machine to provide both guns and butter. The root of the bloc's economic troubles was not inefficiency alone, but the fact that the continuous modernization of its vast armed forces was bleeding it to death.

Stealth threatened to render a great deal of that hardware obsolete, and to demand yet another cycle of modernization, probably a costlier one than ever before. It was another turn of an unbearably tight screw. It may not be too much to say that the F-117 has already accomplished its most valuable mission; it helped knock a chunk out of the Wall.

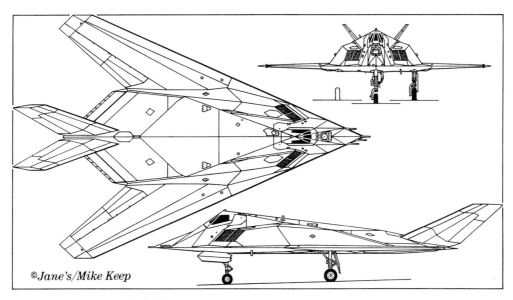

©Jane's/Mike Keep

F-117A Data

Dimensions

Wingspan	43 ft 4 in	(13.21 m)
Length overall	65 ft 11 in	(20.09 m)
Body length	55 ft 1 in	(16.78 m)
Height	12 ft 5 in	(3.78 m)
Wing/body area	1070 sq ft	(100 sq m)

Powerplant

Two General Electric F404–F1D2 nonafterburning engines

Thrust	10,600 lb	(47.1 kN)
Bypass ratio	0.34:1	
Weight	1,820 lb	(825 kg)

Weights

Max take-off	52,500 lb	(23,810 kg)
Internal fuel	13,000 lb	(5,895 kg)
Weapon load	4,000 lb	(1,815 kg)
Operating empty	35,000 lb	(15,875 kg)

Estimated performance

Max Mach number	0.95	
Max speed at sea level	560 kt	(1,040 km/h)
Max speed at 35,000 ft	545 kt	(1,010 km/h)
Cruising speed	460 kt	(850 km/h)
Combat radius*	500 nm	(930 km)

*"Unlimited" with inflight refueling

F-117A production

The US Air Force provided a complete listing of F-117A serial numbers as this book closed for press. This list confirmed that fifty-nine production aircraft were built, not counting the five full-scale development (FSD) aircraft. In all, sixty-four F-117s were built. In mid 1990, fifty-six operational aircraft were in the USAF inventory; of the five FSD aircraft, some are probably in storage and others may be engaged in tests of F-117 improvements and modifications.

The initial batch of twenty production aircraft were built at a rate of ten per year. The last of these was delivered in June 1984. The rate decreased to eight aircraft per year for the next three years and then began to taper off, as no further aircraft were authorized.

According to the USAF, the F-117As are identified in a non standard series of three-digit serial numbers used for some special programs. They do not carry standard USAF serials: 787, for example, is not an abbreviation of 80-0787 as one might expect.

Production	Serial	Acceptance date	Remarks
FSD	780	Not available	
FSD	781	Not available	
FSD	782	Not available	
FSD	783	Not available	
FSD	784	Not available	
1	785	Lost before acceptance	Lost April 20, 1982
2	786	Sept. 2, 1982	
3	787	Aug. 23, 1982	
4	788	Oct. 22, 1982	
5	789	Nov. 17, 1982	
6	790	Dec. 11, 1982	
7	791	Dec. 13, 1982	
8	792	Dec. 22, 1982	Lost June 11, 1986
9	793	Feb. 1, 1983	
10	794	April 15, 1983	
11	795	Sept. 9, 1983	
12	796	Aug. 4, 1983	
13	797	Aug. 31, 1983	
14	798	Oct. 3, 1983	

Production	Serial	Acceptance date	Remarks
15	799	Oct. 28, 1983	4450 TG declared operational
16	800	Dec. 7, 1983	
17	801	Feb. 15, 1984	
18	802	April 6, 1984	
19	803	June 22, 1984	
20	804	June 20, 1984	Last aircraft of initial batch
21	805	Aug. 3, 1984	
22	806	Sept. 12, 1984	
23	807	Nov. 28, 1984	
24	808	Dec. 20, 1984	
25	809	April 16, 1985	
26	810	Feb. 14, 1985	
27	811	March 29, 1985	
28	812	June 12, 1985	
29	813	July 10, 1985	
30	814	Sept. 5, 1985	
31	815	Oct. 31, 1985	Lost Oct. 14,1987
32	816	Dec. 20, 1985	
33	817	Feb. 28, 1986	
34	818	May 22, 1986	
35	819	April 24, 1986	
36	820	June 19, 1986	
37	821	Aug. 1, 1986	
38	822	Sept. 18, 1986	
39	823	Dec. 4, 1986	
40	824	Dec. 17, 1986	
41	825	March 25, 1987	
42	826	March 25, 1987	
43	827	May 18, 1987	
44	828	June 17, 1987	
45	829	Nov. 27, 1987	
46	830	Nov. 27, 1987	
47	831	Nov. 27, 1987	
48	832	Feb. 11, 1988	
49	833	May 25, 1988	
50	834	May 27, 1988	
51	835	Aug. 15, 1988	
52	836	Oct. 19, 1988	
53	837	Feb. 22, 1989	
54	838	May 24, 1989	
55	839	Aug. 14, 1989	
56	840	Nov. 1, 1989	
57	841	March 8, 1989	
58	842	March 28, 1990	
59	843	July 1990	Not delivered at press-time

Index